My Changing Body

The #1 book for girls on the verge of change.

My Changing Body

Girl's Edition

Linda Picone

Fairview Press
Minneapolis

Published by Fairview Press, 2450 Riverside Avenue, Minneapolis, MN 55454. For a free catalog of Fairview Press titles, call toll-free 1-800-544-8207, or visit our website at www.fairviewpress.org.

Fairview Press is a division of Fairview Health Services, a community-focused health system, affiliated with the University of Minnesota, providing a complete range of services, from the prevention of illness and injury to care for the most complex medical conditions.

Library of Congress Cataloging-in-Publication Data
Picone, Linda.
 My changing body : girl's edition : the #1 book for girls on the verge of change / Linda Picone.
    p. cm.
 ISBN 978-1-57749-187-3 (alk. paper)
 1. Puberty—Juvenile literature. 2. Teenage girls—Juvenile
literature. I. Title.
 QP84.4.P533 2010
 612.6'61—dc22

                    2009041700

Book design by Ryan Scheife, Mayfly Design (www.mayflydesign.net)
Cover illustration © 2009 by Jeanine Henderson
Interior illustrations by Bruce A. Wilson (www.brucewilsonart.com)

Printed in Canada
First printing: April 2010

14   13   12   11   10   7   6   5   4   3   2   1

Contents

Introduction

Growing Up

Some days you can't wait to grow up. Other times, you wish you could just stay a kid forever. You want to learn how to drive, to be able to make more decisions for yourself, to know what you are going to look like when you become an adult. But you also like the feeling of being taken care of by your parents and knowing that you can make mistakes without it being a big deal.

Many changes take place on the inside and the outside of your body as you change from girl into a young adult woman. These changes are natural and normal, but they can also be mysterious and even scary. Why is your body doing *that*? What does it mean? When will it stop? What will you be like after these changes?

Your parents, teachers, and other trusted adults can help you understand what happens to your body as you grow up. To talk to them and to ask good questions, you need to know the words—the correct words—that describe your body and the things you are feeling. This book lets you find the correct words, and it tells you about the changes that are part of growing up.

How to Read This Book

You can read this book in a couple of different ways:

1. You can read each chapter to learn about different aspects of growing up. You'll see some words in **boldface**. You can find a short definition for these words in the dictionary at the end of the book.
2. You can go to the dictionary to find out what a particular word means, whether or not you read the rest of the book.

You probably will read a little bit at a time. Maybe you want to know what happens to girls as they grow up, because you are a girl. Maybe you want to know about how babies grow and are born. Maybe you are interested in what it means to date someone. It is fine to go to any chapter you want. You don't have to read the chapters in order.

When you have questions, look for the answers in this book but remember that your parents know a lot about growing up, too. They were kids once themselves!

Words You Can't Say in Front of Your Parents

The kind of slang words or dirty words you hear at school or in movies aren't in this book, because:

1. We want you to think about your body in a good way. Slang words often say ugly things about people's bodies.
2. Slang words change all the time. They can mean one thing today and a different thing tomorrow. People may use one word in Texas and a completely different word in New Hampshire for exactly the same thing.

3. You should learn the real word for each body part, emotion, or action.

You may hear words you don't know and want to look up what they mean. Ask your parents, guardians, or a friend you trust for the real word so that you can read about it in the dictionary part of this book.

For Parents and Guardians

You are your children's most important teachers. They learn from what you say and, even more important, from what you do. If you dodge their questions about how their bodies are changing and what it means, they get the message: It's something they're supposed to be embarrassed about. If you listen and try to help them understand their new physical and emotional selves, they learn something quite different: They're growing up and it may be kind of strange, but it's okay; everyone goes through it.

We encourage you to use this book as a tool to help in those talks with your children—not as a substitute for such conversations. The narrative part of each chapter tells how our bodies work in childhood, adolescence, and adulthood, and helps your children understand their feelings, sense of self, and relationships with others (including their parents). The dictionary provides accurate, science-based definitions of common and not-so-common terms.

No book can substitute for parental guidance on moral, religious, and philosophical values about relationships, sexuality, families, and what it means to be a person in our culture. Your children need to talk to *you*. We hope you will respond when they ask questions—and start the conversation even if they don't.

1

Basic Anatomy: Is This Still Me?

You can't always tell a boy **baby** from a girl baby when you look at them. They may have the same kind of hair. Or no hair! The same chubby faces, the same arms and legs and tummies. Sometimes the only way you can tell boy babies and girl babies apart is by their clothes.

Under their diapers, girl babies and boy babies are different, but for about the first nine or ten years of their lives, everything else is pretty much the same. Kids grow and get taller, but the main way we tell boys and girls apart is by what they wear, their haircuts, their names, and what they like to do.

Then it all changes.

Maybe all of a sudden you are a lot taller than you used to be and your clothes don't fit right. Maybe you've got hair growing in places you never had hair. You sweat more. Your skin is breaking out.

All normal.

Or maybe none of those things are happening to you yet, but you look around and your friends seem to be changing.

That's normal, too.

That's Why They Call Them the "Awkward Years"

Sometime between your eighth and fifteenth birthday, you begin the kinds of changes that will turn you into an adult. This time of your life is called **adolescence**. Your body starts becoming more like an adult body. You also feel different. Not like an adult, but definitely not like a little kid anymore.

Another word for these changes is **puberty**. Adolescence and puberty are pretty much the same, but some people use the word puberty to talk about the way your body is changing and the word adolescence to talk about how your feelings are changing, along with your body.

Girls usually begin puberty between nine and eleven years old—although some may start earlier and some later. Boys usually begin puberty a year or so later than girls. Everyone is on his or her own schedule. You and your friends and classmates start to look very different during adolescence. Some of you get taller and start to seem more adult. Others are still pretty much like kids.

Look at yourself, your friends, and your classmates. How many different sizes and shapes do you see?

Puberty lasts for a few years. Some kids go through it quickly and have adult bodies even before they go to high school. Others may still be growing and changing when they start college.

One way to figure out when you are likely to start puberty and how long it will take is to ask your parents about their adolescence. If your mom says she starting wearing a bra and having periods when she was eleven, you might start adolescence early, too.

It can feel weird to be the shortest kid in your class. Or the tallest. Or to have breasts before any of your girlfriends do. Sometimes it seems like "feeling weird" is what adolescence is all about. Besides the changes happening to your body, there may be a lot of changes in the way you feel about yourself or your family or your friends. In fact, the way you feel about pretty much everything may change, at least for a while.

Talk to your parents or other adults about what adolescence was like for them. Ask if they ever felt "different." How did they handle it?

Body Basics

Your body is made up of several systems, or groups of parts. They work together to let you do everything from breathing to walking to thinking. If you know how your body works, you can understand how it changes in adolescence.

There are a lot of differences between a man's body and a woman's body, but the basic structure is the same. Everything in your body starts with a **cell**. Cells are the smallest part of any living being. They are called the "building blocks of life." In your body, groups of cells make up organs, like the heart or lungs, plus different **body fluids**, including blood and **mucus**. In fact, you got started from one cell in your mother's body (more about that in Chapter 8). Everyone's body is made up of the following systems:

- **Skeletal system.** From your head (skull) to the tips of your toes, your bones hold everything in your body. Bones protect your important organs. Muscles attach to the bones so that you can move. Some bones make blood.
- **Cardiovascular system.** Your heart and blood, plus the arteries and veins that carry blood, make up your cardiovascular system. The heart pumps blood into the arteries and sends it all through your body. This

is important because your blood carries oxygen and
other important things to all of your cells. Veins let the
blood move back to the heart, which moves it through
your lungs so it can pick up oxygen.

- **Digestive system.** The food you eat goes through several stages in your digestive system so that the important material from your food can be broken down and
go into your cells. Your digestive system starts with
your mouth, then down through a long tube called
the esophagus, to the stomach, the small intestine,
the large intestine, and then to the rectum and **anus.**
Food gets broken down, or digested, in the stomach.
The good parts of digested food, called nutrients, go
through the intestinal walls and go to other parts of
your body. Other organs in your digestive system are
the gallbladder, pancreas, and liver.

- **Muscular system.** Muscles let you move. Muscles are
connected to bones. When they get a signal from your
brain, the cells in a muscle pull together and something moves. Some muscles move only when you give
them a signal, like when you want to close your fingers
to pick something up. Others, like your heart or lungs,
move without you telling them to.

- **Nervous system.** You have tiny strings of nerve cells
everywhere in your body. They carry messages about
everything, from breathing to feeling pain. Your brain
and spinal cord are the center of your nervous system.

- **Urinary system.** When blood has taken nutrients and
oxygen through your body, some waste material is left
over. Your urinary system filters out that waste material in the kidneys (you have two of them). Then it
travels through the **ureters** and is stored in the **bladder.**

When your bladder gets full and you need to use the bathroom, the urine leaves your body through the **urethra**. It comes out of your **urinary opening**, which is different in men and women.

- **Reproductive system.** Men and women have very different **reproductive organs**. These are the organs that let a baby get started, grow, and then be born. Chapter 3 tells how the female reproductive system works.

- **Endocrine system.** Your nervous system controls most things that happen quickly in your body, like signaling muscles to move. Another system, your endocrine system, gives your body the signals it needs to do things that happen slowly, like growing or changing. The endocrine system is made of **glands** that make or give off chemicals that send messages to different cells in your body.

Magic Messengers

The chemicals your glands produce are called **hormones**. Some hormones make you sweat. Other hormones make you grow hair. Others make you feel happy or sad.

Hormones cause most of what happens to you in adolescence. You may hear people complaining about hormones going crazy in teenagers. They're not going crazy. They're doing exactly what they're supposed to. Some glands and hormones start doing new things during adolescence.

- **Sweat glands** make your body sweat, which is one way it stays at the right temperature. They start working harder when you get to puberty.

- The tiny **pituitary gland**—it's about the size of a pea— helps control your growth. The hormones it gives off are important to your reproductive organs.

- You have **sebaceous glands** everywhere except the palms of your hands and the bottoms of your feet. The sebaceous glands give off **sebum**, an oily substance that helps keep your skin and hair from getting too dry. You need sebum, but if you get too much, or if a sebaceous gland gets clogged, it can cause skin or hair problems.

Signs of Change

Some of the first signs that you're in adolescence are the same whether you're a boy or a girl, but the biggest changes are very different. We'll talk more about those big changes in the next couple of chapters.

Up, Up, Up

Of course you've been growing every since you were a baby, but you might find you're outgrowing your clothes really quickly now. You may have a **growth spurt,** which just means that what you think is happening really *is* happening—you're getting taller very fast. The average boy grows as much as eleven inches—nearly a foot!—during puberty. But puberty can go on for a long time for boys, so they might not get to their full height until they're out of high school. Girls don't grow as much, but you grow earlier than boys—many girls are as tall as they will ever be by the time they are fifteen.

When and how you grow taller depend a lot on your parents—and their parents and brothers and sisters, too. If both of your parents are tall, chances are you will be, too. If both are shorter, you're likely to be shorter. If your mother is short, but her mother (your grandmother) is tall, you might be short, tall, or somewhere in between.

There's not much you can do to make yourself taller. Keeping yourself healthy with good foods (more vegetables than candy!) and exercise can help you make sure you get to the full height you should be.

Some parts of your body may grow faster than others, so you feel kind of clumsy. Big feet trip over every pebble. Long legs don't know how to walk in a straight line anymore. Growing up doesn't always happen neatly.

Whether you're shorter or taller than you want to be, stand up straight and proud. You look your best when you seem happy with yourself.

Make a "growth tree"—like a family tree, but with everyone's adult heights filled in. Ask your parents and grandparents when they got to be as tall as they are now.

Spotty Problems

When you're a little kid, your skin is soft and clear, no matter what you do to it. But oops, now it's different. Just when you really start to care about how you look, your skin may start getting **pimples** or **zits** (they're the same thing). They can look like white spots or black dots or turn into big red sores. You might have a few around your nose, forehead, or chin, or you might have them all over your face. **Acne** is a lot of pimples that don't go away easily. Some kids are lucky and don't get any pimples, but most have at least a few.

When you have a pimple, you think *everyone* is looking at you. It's hard to feel good about yourself when you're sure you've got a HUGE red spot right there, where everyone can see it.

Luckily, there are ways to help with pimples:

- **Keep it clean.** Pimples start under your skin, but they get worse because of dirt and bacteria on the surface of your skin. Keeping your skin clean helps keep pimples from getting worse. Wash your face twice a day with a mild soap and warm (not superhot) water. Don't wash too often or too hard—that can make your skin break out more. You can find special soaps for dealing with pimples, but you don't have to have anything special. Don't use a deodorant soap on your face. They're meant only for your body.

- **Hands off!** Pimples can itch or hurt and you just want to scratch or squeeze them to make it stop. That's the worst thing you can do. Squeezing a pimple won't get rid of it. It's more likely to make things a lot worse. One little pimple can turn into a really ugly sore and then leave a scar if you fuss with it.

- **Try the drugstore.** You can find creams, gels, and lotions to attack the zits, and oil-free cover-ups and makeup to help hide them. Ask your friends, parents, a pharmacist, or others for advice on what might work best for you. Don't overdo it! Using too much stuff or using it too often can damage your skin. Heavy make-up can draw attention to your pimples.

- **See a doctor.** Some people see a doctor even for mild acne. There are prescription products you use on your skin that are stronger than anything you can buy off the shelf. If you have a lot of pimples, or pimples that just won't go away, a dermatologist (the kind of doctor who treats skin problems) may prescribe medication you take by mouth to fight the acne from inside your body.

- **Smile.** The most important thing others see on your face is your expression. If you try to hide yourself because your pimples embarrass you, you look worse. Put on a big smile. It's the best "makeup" you can find.

Sweaty and Smelly

Even babies sweat when they get hot or when they exercise. As you go into adolescence, you start to sweat for what can seem like no reason at all. You're embarrassed or nervous and suddenly you feel damp under your armpits and on your forehead. You feel sweat in places you never felt it before, like between your legs.

When you go into puberty, you sweat more, and you have a different kind of sweat in some places. Sweat or **perspiration** is mostly just water. When it comes through your skin and the air dries it off, you feel cooler. Once you start puberty, the sweat in your armpits, around your **groin** (between your legs), and on your **nipples** (boys and girls) also has tiny bits of cell material in it. The watery part just disappears into the air, but the tiny bits of cell stay on your skin and can start to smell bad, giving you **body odor**.

Adolescents can get pretty stinky if they don't take care of themselves. Having good **hygiene** and taking care of yourself are pretty easy, though.

- **Wash.** Don't let the tiny bits of cell build up on your body. Take showers or baths regularly, especially after exercising, and wash your armpits and groin area well.
- **Put on clean clothes.** It doesn't matter if your body is clean if you put on clothes that already have sweat on them. Give your clothes a good hard sniff before putting them on. If they smell bad, so will you.
- **Use deodorants or antiperspirants.** Deodorants help keep you smelling better, but don't stop you from sweating. Antiperspirants have a stronger effect. They

make you sweat less. Both usually are made with chemicals and can cause problems for some people. Even if you use a deodorant or antiperspirant, you need to start with a clean body.

Hair Where?

For a lot of kids, growing hair in new places—and more hair in some old places—is one of the first signs of puberty.

You may have had very light, thin hair on your arms and legs even as a little kid. Now that hair is darker and thicker. Hair starts to grow near your groin, on the **pudendum**, the slight bump right in front. This is called **pubic hair**. Hair grows in your armpits. Boys start to get hair on their faces. (Girls might also find some darker hairs on their faces, especially on the upper lip.) Boys may get hair on their chests, and girls may find a few hairs around their nipples.

Some people end up with a lot of hair, some with barely any. People fuss about hair a lot. Girls may panic over a tiny "moustache." (Did you know that some cultures consider hair on a woman's upper lip very attractive?)

Take a look at your parents and any older brothers or sisters. Chances are your hair will be something like theirs.

What's Happening?

Ways your body may be changing:

- You're getting taller.
- Your skin is breaking out.
- You sweat more.
- You have hair growing in new places.

2

New Emotions and Identity: Becoming Who You Are

Adolescence is not easy. There are so many things going on:

- Your body is changing (see Chapter 1) and it takes time to get used to hair in new places, growing taller (or not growing while everyone else seems to be), zits on your face, breasts . . . Whose body is this, anyway?
- Your family and teachers are telling you that everything counts now. Getting a bad grade or fooling around in school didn't used to seem that important. Now you're thinking about high school and what happens after high school, and everything you do seems to matter a lot.
- You're starting to have different feelings about almost everything, including your family, your friends, yourself. Your life used to seem so easy and now it just isn't.

You're Up, You're Down, You're Confused

The same hormones that make your body change also can affect the way you feel. And wow, do you feel! You are the happiest person in the world one moment. An hour later—or just a few minutes later—you want to curl up in a ball and cry. All of your **emotions** are so strong, you sometimes think you can hardly stand it.

You may yell at your brother and sister. They are *so* annoying. You're rude to your parents. You get angry with your best friend and say something hurtful.

Or you may be so happy that you want to kiss everyone in your house. You feel like you don't need to eat or sleep. All you want to do is listen to your favorite song played VERY LOUD while you dance around the room.

With all of those things going on in your head, it's no wonder that sometimes you act crazy. You might get angry or mean and snap at people when they're just being themselves. You might feel sad and try to lock yourself in your room for hours. You might feel just kind of nuts. You bounce from one thing to another. You can't seem to stick to anything for very long.

In the Mood

Mood swings are a normal part of adolescence. If you understand this, you can handle them better. The way you feel may seem like something you can't control, but there are ways to cope and to keep yourself a little more settled:

- **Stop a moment.** Whether you are really happy or really angry or really sad, take a little time just to think about how you're feeling. Make a promise to yourself that you will count to at least ten before you say or do anything because of your strong feelings.

- **Eat a healthy diet.** Some teens seem to live on coffee, diet soda, candy, and junk food. Or they skip meals, then pig out later. You already know that's not good for you, but you may not know that kind of diet also can affect your moods.

- **Get plenty of sleep.** You may talk to your friends on the computer or the phone until way past midnight, then get up early to head off to school. It seems like you can handle it, but your body needs plenty of energy as it's growing and changing—and that means it needs plenty of sleep, too. It's easy to blow up or feel really down when you are just plain tired.

- **Exercise.** If your emotions are so strong you just feel like you have to explode somehow, get moving. Go for a run or a bike ride. Do aerobics. Dance like crazy. Or just take a nice, long walk. As you exercise, good hormones are sent through your body, making you feel nice and mellow.

- **Talk to someone you trust.** It's important to have someone you can really talk to, who will help you understand what's happening to your body and your emotions. Your friends can be good listeners, but they don't have the kind of experience you need sometimes. If you don't feel like you can talk to your parents or guardians, find another adult you think understands you. Maybe a teacher, maybe an uncle or aunt who's always been there for you, maybe a coach or someone from your religious group.

Do you have someone you can talk to when you need a reality check? Find an adult you trust and start talking to that person regularly, before you need help.

Most young people have a lot of ups and downs, but sometimes they can be more than just a normal part of growing up. If you start feeling like you can't handle things by yourself, don't be afraid to ask for help. It's important to reach out to a responsible adult when you are in trouble.

Liking Your Body

As your body changes, you start to pay a lot of attention to how you look—and how you *think* you're supposed to look. It doesn't help when you see pictures of models and stars who seem to be perfect. No extra pounds, hair that behaves, great skin, long legs. You might compare yourself to the best-looking girl you know, or to an actor or model, whose job it is to look amazing. Those comparisons only make you feel bad about yourself. (Even movie stars aren't perfect. They just look like they are thanks to makeup and personal trainers and some computer "magic.")

Feeling good about yourself starts with liking your own body. After all, your body gets you from place to place and lets you enjoy things like the warm sun on your skin or the taste of your favorite ice cream or the sound of your friends laughing.

Instead of thinking about the parts of your body you don't like, think about what you *do* like. Maybe it's your strong legs or your curly hair or the color of your eyes. Some things about your body can be changed a little. If you're heavier than most young people your age, you can lose weight by exercising and eating in a healthy way. If your skin is breaking out, you can keep it clean and use medication to help clear it up. A good haircut can make your hair look its best, no matter how curly or straight it is.

You can't change everything about yourself. If you're taller than other people, you're probably going to be taller for the rest of your life. If you're shorter, you may still grow, but you could stay shorter than most other people. The basic shape of your body is probably going to stay the same, even as you get older. Learn to like that body just the way it is.

Stand in front of a big mirror and look hard at yourself.
Tell yourself what you like and why.

If you like your body, other people will see that. When you stand up straight, walk proud, and have a big smile on your face, you look good.

Other People in Your Life

While you're having all these strong and confusing emotions, you may find you feel differently about the people around you, from your family to your friends.

What's Wrong with Your Parents?

As a child, you wanted to be with your parents all the time and have them tell you how wonderful you were. You thought they were wonderful, too. Now you may get embarrassed by almost everything they do. One day you can't wait to just get away from them. The next day you wish you could curl up in your mom's or dad's lap, just like you did when you were little.

Most people have some ups and downs while they're changing from a child to an adult. A baby bird learns to fly and leave the nest in just a few days, but people take years to make the change. You still need adults in your life to protect you, teach you, and guide you. At the same time, you are trying new things and want to see how much you can do on your own. Many young people feel as if they can do anything they want, without getting hurt or hurting others. It's hard to listen to adults who tell you something is dangerous or not good for you. Try to remember that growing up doesn't happen all at once. You have years to learn how to be an adult. Don't rush it.

Be a Friend

You and your friends may be changing at different speeds and in different ways during adolescence. If your best friend's body and ideas change faster than yours, you may feel like he or she has left you behind. If you are the one changing faster, you may feel that your friend is too babyish now.

It's normal to find your friendships changing. Maybe you barely talk to someone who was your best friend just a year ago. Losing friends can hurt. You wonder if there's something wrong with you—or them. Chances are it's just a part of growing up, and you'll find yourself making new friends as some of the older friends go out of your life. If you feel like you have no friends, or you have a hard time making new friends, or you just feel very bad about yourself, talk to an adult or older teen you trust. They can remind you that you're a good person. They also can give you tips for getting along with others:

- **Be friendly.** You'd be surprised how many other young people are nervous about others. Just like you, they worry that someone else will make fun of them or say something mean to them. Think how much you would like it if someone simply was friendly to you when you were feeling shy. Put a smile on your face and go out and meet others.

- **Do things you like.** If you run, join the track team. If you are great at argument, join the debate team. Take part in activities related to your religion. Join the Girl Scouts or 4-H or other clubs. It's easier to make friends when you're doing something you like—and so are they.

- **Have different kinds of friends.** You don't have to have just one or two friends to do everything with. It's good to have a number of friends. Maybe the person you really like to hang out with on the swim team doesn't like the same kinds of movies you do, but another friend is great to go to the movies with. Having more friends lets you find out what you like to do.
- **Don't do mean things.** That sounds simple and kind of silly, but some young people turn into bullies just because they don't feel good about themselves. If they can make someone else feel bad, they think they will show that they're more important. Bullying is not just hurting someone by fighting or hitting. You can be a bully using words.
- **Let people count on you.** If you tell a friend you'll do something with her or him, do it. Call when you say you will call. Be there if a friend needs to talk. Pay attention to what's happening in other people's lives and let them know you care about them.
- **Pay attention to what others do.** Look at the people you want as friends and see what it is about them that others seem to like, too. Don't be a copycat, but see if there are some things you are missing.

As much as you want to make friends, remember to be yourself. No one else is just like you, and that's a good thing. Your friends should like the real you, not someone pretending to be like them.

Because friends are so important during your growing-up years, you might find yourself doing things that don't feel right, just to get along with your group. Other young people may push you to try drugs or alcohol, or to steal things from stores or to be mean to someone else. You know these kinds of things aren't good for you, but you're afraid that if you don't do them, your friends will drop you. This kind of **peer pressure** can happen at any time in your life, but it's especially strong during adolescence.

Having a big circle of friends can help. If one group seems to be pressuring you to do something you don't like, you can spend more time with other friends. If you feel like you're being pushed into things you don't feel good about, or that you know your family would dislike, try to talk to an adult who will understand and help you do the right thing.

That old saying, "Be the friend you want," makes a lot of sense. Think about the kind of people you like—and then act like them.

Ideas about Sex

Until your body starts changing, you don't think all that much about whether your friends are boys or girls or both. Now, all of that is kind of mixed up. You may be a girl who still likes to hang out with boys, but some of the boys are treating you in a funny way. Or you're a girl who sees other girls spending a lot of time talking about boys, talking to boys, and worrying about their looks, and you just don't get it.

During adolescence, you start to think about something more than friendship with some people. As your body changes, you get interested in being close to another person. You may think about having a boyfriend, or just talking and being close to someone.

The problem is that everyone starts having these feelings at a slightly different time. If you get interested in boys earlier than the rest of your friends, they may wonder what's going on with you. If you are not interested, but your friends start going on dates or hanging out hoping to get close to boys, you may feel left behind—and you may think your friends are just kind of silly.

What's happening to you or your friends is one of the first steps to learning about **sex**. Sex is the way human beings get together and have babies, but it's also much more. Two people who care about each other can become closer because they have sex. (More about sex in Chapter 4.)

We use the word "sex" in several ways. Sometimes we use it as a way to indicate the difference between a man (**male**) and woman (**female**). A better word for that purpose is **gender**. Sex also means what two people do together to be close.

Becoming Sexual

Even before you are born, you have the **sex organs** of a male or female. This means that if you are a female, you have a **uterus**, **vagina**, and other organs designed to support and grow a baby. If you are a male, you have a **penis** and **testicles** to help make a baby. The sex organs that show on the outside of your body are also called your **genitals** or **genitalia**. These **sexual characteristics** are the biological difference between a man and a woman.

As you become an adolescent, you start to develop **secondary sexual characteristics**, like the hair under your arms, breasts, curvier hips, or other things that we think of as being part of being a woman.

Sometimes we talk about someone as being **sexy**, which usually means they seem to signal that they want to have sex—or at least to get very physical. A sexy woman might show off her breasts or her legs. A sexy man might talk to women a certain way that seems to invite them to be close. **Sexuality** is the way you feel about your body and the way you connect with other people. You have sexuality, even if you don't think about yourself as being sexy.

Male or Female?

Besides our sex organs, what we do tells others whether we are male or female. Some people have very strict ideas about how a man is supposed to behave, or how a woman is supposed to behave. They may think the proper **sex role** for a woman is to raise children and take care of the family and the correct sex role for a man is to support his family and to be strong.

Sex roles today are not that strict. Many women support their families and many men are proud of the way they raise their children. Some men and women never get married or have children, but they are still very much male or female. They know their **gender identity** from the moment they are old enough to understand the word "girl" or "boy." You may be a tomboy and enjoy sports, but you know you are a girl.

Once in a while, a girl or boy can feel like she or he is in the wrong body. A girl can have female genitalia, but something inside her tells her she is the other gender. These feelings are very hard for such people, especially as they are growing up. The rest of the world sees them as one gender, but they just don't feel that way. **Transgender** means that someone's gender identity doesn't match his or her sex organs. Some transgender people have surgery when they are adults so that their bodies can match what they feel.

What's Happening?

Ways your feelings may be changing:

- Your moods go up and down and up and down.
- You're worrying a lot about how you look.
- You love your parents—but sometimes you just can't stand them.
- You and your friends aren't getting along the same as you used to.
- You're experiencing new feelings about boys.

3

The Female Body: Becoming a Woman

A girl's body is a little mysterious—most guys *and* girls would agree with that. A female has more parts to her reproductive system than a male and most of her parts are inside the body, so they seem hidden. If you read history, you will see that women's bodies often are seen as magical—because they are able to grow and give **birth** to babies. When a girl goes through puberty, she changes into a woman. That means her body becomes ready to have babies—even though her life is not yet ready for them.

Stages of Puberty for Girls

There are several female hormones that tell your body to start changing from a girl to a woman. **Estrogen** is the most important, but **progesterone** and **prostaglandin** also make your female sex organs develop and your **breasts** grow.

Girls tend to go into puberty earlier than boys. You already may be taller and older looking than boys who are your same age. There are five stages of puberty for girls:

- Stage One, usually from eight to eleven years old.
  You can't see anything happening on the outside, but
  inside, female hormones are increasing.
- Stage Two, usually from eight to fourteen years old.
  Your chest, which used to be flat, is starting to grow
  bumps. You might grow taller and heavier. You see a
  little hair in your pubic area.
- Stage Three, usually from nine to fifteen years old. The
  bumps on your chest are getting bigger and there is
  more pubic hair, which usually is darker than the first
  hairs you see. You may get your first **menstrual period**
  during this stage.
- Stage Four, usually from ten to sixteen years old. You
  now have some hair under your arms and more pubic
  hair. You may have some menstrual periods, but they
  aren't regular yet.
- Stage Five, usually from twelve to nineteen years old.
  Your body is an adult body by the end of this stage
  (even if you don't feel or act like an adult). The bumps
  on your chest are full breasts, and your pubic hair
  covers the pubic area. You have regular monthly menstrual periods. You probably are as tall as you're going
  to be.

Every girl goes through puberty a little differently. A fourteen-
year-old girl could be in Stage Two, Stage Three, or even Stage
Four. You and your friends may look very different from each
other during this time. If you're developing faster than your
friends or other girls your age, you may feel out of place or
strange—and if you're developing more slowly, you may feel the
same thing. Just remember: you're all going to end up with womanly bodies before long.

When did you start puberty and how long were you in each stage, until you got to where you are now? Keep a record for yourself.

A Woman's Body

Although there's a lot going on inside your body as you go through puberty, the first things you see will be changes in the shape of your body. You become womanly, with curves and round places where you used to be flat. Your breasts grow and you have a **bosom.**

Breasts

When they're little, boys and girls both have flat chests with two flat **nipples.** As girls go into puberty, the area around their nipples starts to fill out and they develop breasts. Breasts are **mammary glands,** meaning they are special glands designed to make **milk** to feed babies.

You first notice your breasts poking up just a little and forming small "buds." The nipples also start to get just a little bigger, and the areas around the nipples, the **areolae** (the plural form of areola), grow larger. Through puberty, your breasts get rounder and bigger, and the areolae grow larger and may get darker.

Women's breasts are kind of like snowflakes: each one is different. There are big round breasts and small round breasts, but there also are big breasts that look more like pears. Some breasts seem to point up; others seem to point down a little. One breast—usually the left one—can be a little bigger than the other one. Nipples are very different, too. Some women have small areolae that are pink or peach or brown or any color in between; others have big areolae that cover quite a bit of the breast tip.

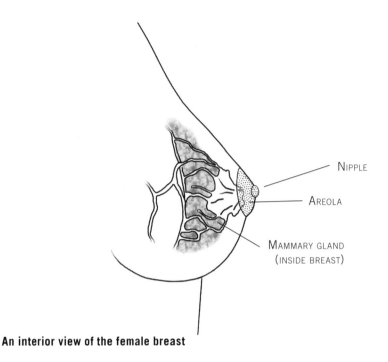

NIPPLE

AREOLA

MAMMARY GLAND
(INSIDE BREAST)

An interior view of the female breast

How big your breasts will be and what shape they will be
depend mostly on what the women in your family look like. If
your mother has large breasts, you probably will, too. If she has
smaller breasts, you may as well. Look at your mother and both
grandmothers if you want to see what your breasts *might* look
like when they've finished growing.

Girls—and women—worry a lot about what their breasts
look like. If you have big breasts, you may get attention you don't
want from boys. If you have small breasts, you may think you
don't look attractive. Your breasts are just what they are supposed
to be for your body. All sizes and shapes can look attractive, if
you wear the right clothing and bras.

GOOD SUPPORT

Some girls want to wear a bra the minute they see a breast bud. Others try to put off getting a bra as long as they can. You don't *have* to wear a bra until you can feel your breasts jiggle and bounce when you walk, or when you can feel the nipples rub against your shirt. But you might *want* to wear a bra just to fit in with your friends, or to make sure the way your breasts are growing is private—not something everyone can see. There are "training" bras that help cover up new breast buds when you need them. Once your breasts are more developed, you may be more comfortable wearing a bra that fits than going without a bra.

When you go to buy a bra, try on quite a few so that you know what fits best. An adult you trust can help, and most department stores have saleswomen who are trained to help women find the right bra. Yes, that can be a little embarrassing, but you won't be the first young teen who's asked for help, and having a bra that fits right is worth a few minutes of feeling weird.

THINGS YOU MAY SEE

- **Stretch marks.** Some girls' breasts grow very quickly. As they grow, the skin is stretched and you may get reddish **stretch marks**. These are nothing to worry about. They are likely to fade over time and you will barely be able to see them. You can use a cream or moisturizer to help keep your skin moist so that it will stretch a little more easily.
- **Hair.** Some women have a few hairs around their nipples. If you see a few hairs, you can use tweezers to pluck them, but don't try to shave them or use a hair-removing cream. Your areolae and nipples are very sensitive, and a sharp blade or strong chemical could hurt you.

- **Leaking.** Because your breasts are made to give milk to a baby, they may leak a little while they are growing. If the leaking (called **discharge**) is white, clear, or a light color, don't worry about it. If it looks like it has blood in it or is a dark color, you should see a doctor just to make sure it's not a problem.

The Rest of Your Shape

Usually a woman's body is round and curvy. Even very thin women have curves. As you go through puberty, your curves start to show. Your rear end (or **buttocks**) gets bigger. Some girls have smaller—but still round—buttocks, and others have bigger buttocks. Like breasts, buttocks come in all kinds of different sizes and shapes.

Your pelvis, which is formed by big bones at the bottom of your spine that protect your organs, starts to widen as you go through puberty. Because your body is built to hold a baby, these bones move apart a little, starting in puberty, so there is more room for a baby inside you.

Women have more body fat than girls—or than men. As you go into puberty, you are likely to see more fat on your thighs and your **abdomen**, as well as on your buttocks and breasts. It's normal to have this kind of change in your body. (See Chapter 6 for more about healthy weight.)

All these changes in your body can make you change the way you walk, run, or do other activities. Because you have weight in new places, the way you stand and move is different. You may find that some sports are harder for you now—but others are easier.

Take pictures of yourself, or have a friend take pictures, to show how your body is changing during puberty.

The Things That Make You Female

There's a lot more to you than making babies—and you may never have a baby. But your body is designed to grow a baby inside it, to give birth to it, and then to take care of it once it's born. Babies are created by bringing together a male **sperm cell** and a female **egg cell**, called an **ovum**. The word ovum means "egg" and that's just what it is (**ova** means more than one egg). Sperm and ova come together through sex, but sex for humans is about much more than making babies. It's important to our emotions and our happiness, not just our biology. (More about those topics in Chapters 4 and 5.)

The Egg's Journey

Women have two **ovaries**, each about the size of a large almond or a peach pit. When you were born, you already had about 300,000 cells that can turn into eggs in each ovary. These are all the egg cells your body will make during your lifetime. The number of egg cells goes down a little every day. By the time you are in puberty, you may have about 200,000 in each ovary—more than enough to make a few babies if you want them.

Small spheres (like tiny bags) in your ovaries called **ovarian follicles** make **follicle-stimulating hormone**. This hormone gets egg cells ready to join with male sperm cells. Males have follicles and follicle-stimulating hormones in their testicles that get male sperm cells ready to join with female egg cells.

The **Fallopian tubes** or **oviducts** are the way the egg cells get from the ovaries to the uterus. The egg is moved along through a Fallopian tube (there's one for each ovary) by the movement of tiny **cilia**, which look something like thick hairs. At the end of each Fallopian tube are **fimbriae**, which look like fringe. The fimbriae help eggs move into the **uterus**.

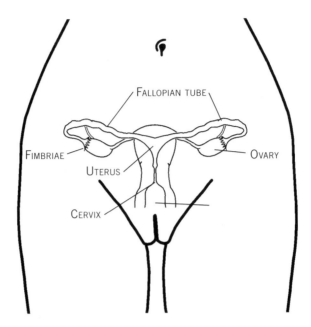

About every twenty-eight days, one egg leaves an ovary and moves into the Fallopian tubes. This is called **ovulation**. Sometimes one ovary lets an egg go, sometimes the other; once in a while, both do.

If a sperm cell meets the egg cell in the Fallopian tubes, a baby is started (we'll talk about how that happens in Chapter 4). If the egg cell doesn't meet a sperm cell—and most of the time, this is what happens—the egg or ovum will just leave your body, as part of your menstrual period.

The **uterus** or **womb** is about the size and shape of a small upside-down pear. The **uterine lining**, called the **endometrium**, grows thicker with rich blood and other material each time an egg cell is released so that a baby can grow in your womb. If the egg cell does not join with a sperm cell, the lining of the uterus comes loose and leaves the body. This is your **menstrual period**. When an egg has joined with a sperm, it settles into the lining of the uterus

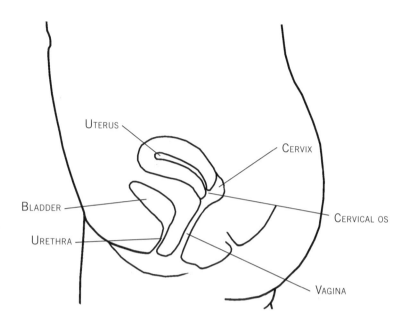

UTERUS

CERVIX

BLADDER

CERVICAL OS

URETHRA

VAGINA

and begins to grow into a baby. The uterus gets bigger as the baby does, growing from pear-sized to watermelon-sized, but it goes back to its original size after the baby is born.

Once you start having periods, your body gets ready to grow a baby every month. Your period is a reminder that your body was designed to make babies—whether or not you ever decide to have one.

At the bottom of your uterus is a narrow space called the **cervix**. Normally, the end of the cervix, called the **os**, is open. If you have a baby growing in your uterus, the cervix gets thick and the **cervical os** closes over so the baby is protected. The cervix has a thick liquid, like a gel, called **cervical mucus** that helps sperm cells move toward an egg cell. The cervical mucus changes during ovulation. You may see cervical mucus in your panties (it will just seem like discharge), especially right between your periods.

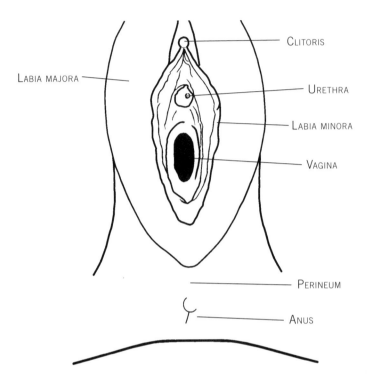

CLITORIS

LABIA MAJORA

URETHRA

LABIA MINORA

VAGINA

PERINEUM

ANUS

From the Inside Out

From the cervix, your body has a kind of tunnel called the **vagina**. This is a baby's entryway to the world during birth, which may happen only a few times during a woman's life. A girl baby is born with a membrane that partly covers the opening of the vagina, called a **hymen**. Some people believe that if you have a hymen, or **maidenhead**, it means you are a **virgin** (have never had sex). But the hymen can get broken without your even knowing it, while you are growing up. It may tear or be stretched open when you are active or playing. If the hymen has not been broken, it will break or stretch open the first time you have sex.

A vagina is only about four inches long and its walls normally are touching—they don't open until something is put in the vagina. **Bartholin's glands,** near the opening of the vagina, and **Skene's glands,** at the upper side of the vagina, make thick fluid or **mucus** that keeps the vagina healthy. It's normal to have a little fluid leak into your panties. Unless it feels itchy or it hurts, don't worry about it.

You can see some of your female body parts, even though most of them are on the inside. The **labia** look like lips, which is what the word "labia" means. There are two sets of labia: an outer pair, called the **labia majora** (or "big lips") and an inner pair, called the **labia minora** (or "little lips).

The labia majora are covered with hair in an adult woman. They hide most of the rest of your sex organs when your legs are together. The labia minora are just inside the labia majora. They are softer, more like folds in your skin.

Just under the labia majora and the labia minora is the **clitoris.** This is a tiny organ, sometimes called a "button" or a "pearl." It is very, very sensitive to any touch, so it has a little piece of covering and protecting it, called the **clitoral hood.** The clitoris is the female version of a man's penis—and the clitoral hood is like a foreskin. The labia and the clitoris together are called the **vulva.**

Males **urinate** and give out sperm through the same tube inside the penis, the **urethra.** The female urethra and vagina are separate. There is a small space near the labia that both the urethra and the vagina open into, called the **vestibule.**

On the outside of your body, the rounded area where your pubic hair grows is the **mons pubis** or **mons veneris.** You can feel the pubic bone right under your skin here.

Between your **anus,** where your bowel movements leave the body, and your vagina is an area called the **perineum.**

Keeping It Clean

The liquid and mucus from your vagina can make you feel a little sticky and you may worry about smelling bad. The normal smell of a woman's sex organs is not bad. It's just a light earthy smell. If you have a sour or strong smell, it may be a sign that you have a problem. See Chapter 6 for more information.

You may see ads for **douches**, which are cleansing solutions that are squirted inside the vagina. These products can cause itching or infection. The liquid your body makes helps keep your vagina clean. You don't need to douche. If you want to clean your vulva:

- Use a mild soap, like baby shampoo. Don't use deodorant soap or soap with perfume in it; these can sting the tender skin or make you itch.
- Gently open the labia and soap yourself, then rinse right away.
- Don't try to clean inside the vagina.
- Pat the vulva area dry.
- Don't use powder or sprays on your vulva or in your panties. These can hurt your skin.

Your "Little Visitor"

Women have had funny names for their menstrual periods for hundreds of years. Sometimes they even call it "the curse." Having periods or **menstruation** is part of being a woman. It can be a little messy and some girls and women have a few problems, but most learn to handle their periods just fine.

Many girls are happy when their periods first begin, because it means they are growing up. Your first period is called **menarche**. You are likely to have your first period sometime between the ages of twelve and thirteen, but it could start when you are as young as nine or as old as sixteen. If you are worried about not starting your periods, ask to see a doctor just to make sure you are okay.

The first time you have a period, you may see spots of blood on your panties. It can be a surprise, especially if it starts when you are not even a teenager yet.

YOUR CYCLE

The time from one period to the next is called your **menstrual cycle**. We talk about the menstrual cycle being twenty-eight days, but that's not true for every woman. Some have a cycle of only twenty-one days; some have cycles as long as forty days. Your periods may not be regular until you've been having them for a couple of years. Between your first periods, you may have a little **spotting**. If it's just a little blood, it's nothing to worry about. If it seems like quite a bit, and it continues for more than a day or two, see a doctor.

To find out what your cycle is, start counting on the first day of your period and then stop counting on the first day of the next period.

Keep track of your periods on a calendar to make sure you know what your cycle is.

Your periods may last for three to seven days. They may start out with just a little blood, then get heavier, then lighter again for the last day or two. The color of the blood may change during your period, from bright red to brownish red. At the heaviest, you will see bits of something that's not quite blood. This is material from your uterus that is coming off because no baby is growing there.

PREMENSTRUAL CRANKINESS

In the week or so just before your period, your hormones are pretty active—and that can be a little uncomfortable for you. You may feel like you are getting heavier, or you may feel some aching in your abdomen. You might get very emotional, sometimes for no reason.

All of these can be part of **premenstrual syndrome** or **PMS**. Not every girl or woman gets PMS, but most have it and some can have a hard time with it. Some of the things you may have just before your period are:

- Headaches
- Sensitive, even painful breasts
- A hard time falling asleep or staying asleep
- Tiredness
- Pimples breaking out
- An achy feeling in your abdomen
- Feeling as if your abdomen is full of air or water (this is called bloating)
- Up and down moods
- Achy muscles or joints

That all sounds pretty bad, but most women and girls don't have many—if any—of these problems. If you are having a lot of problems, or if the problems are very serious, ask to see a doctor. There are medications that help you get through things like headaches or bad cramps.

MENSTRUAL CRAMPS

Most women have an achy feeling when they are having their period. These are **menstrual cramps**. They're not part of PMS because they happen while you are menstruating, not before. For most women, they are a little painful but nothing to worry about. For a few women, though, cramps can be very strong. When you have strong cramps, it's called **dysmenorrhea**. You are more likely to have strong cramps when you are first starting to have your periods.

SELF-HELP

The following are some simple things you can do to make yourself comfortable if you have PMS or during your period:

- **Pain medications.** Aspirin or ibuprofen can help with any pain, whether it's a headache or cramps. Don't take any more than the recommended dose.
- **Heat.** A warm bath or a heating pad on your abdomen can relieve cramps.
- **Exercise.** You may not feel much like running or working out, and you shouldn't overdo it, but a little exercise can help you feel better. Try lying on your back and putting your legs up and moving them as if you were pedaling a bicycle.
- **Sleep.** If you feel tired, achy, and sleepy, well, get to sleep. If you can, go to bed early for a few days until you feel better.

TAKING CARE OF YOUR PERIOD

There are many choices for protecting your clothing and collecting the menstrual blood. **Sanitary napkins** or **pads** come in many sizes and thicknesses. Each one has a sticky strip on the bottom to hold it in place in your panties. (If you are using pads, it works better if you wear regular panties rather than thongs.) Some sanitary napkins are made just for teens, so they fit your body better. You may use different kinds of pads during your period: a thinner, smaller pad when the blood flow is light and a bigger, thicker pad when it's the heaviest.

Change pads as often as you need to stay comfortable (some girls hate the feeling of a wet pad against their body) and clean. When you take a pad out of your panties, wrap it well in toilet tissue and put it in the garbage. Do not flush it.

Tampons are small rolls of cotton or other material that go inside your vagina. As blood comes from your uterus, it's absorbed by the tampon. Some girls don't like the idea of putting something in the vagina.

Some tampons are in plastic or cardboard tubes. To use the tampon, you open your labia and put the tube into your vagina. Push it in until your fingers are against the opening of your vagina. Then push the plunger on the tube slowly and steadily until the tampon is inside. A string will be hanging out of your vagina. If you can feel the tampon inside you, you probably don't have it in the right way. Try again. (Sometimes it's easier to put a tampon in during the heaviest part of your period, because your vagina is slippery then.)

A tampon cannot get lost—the os or opening of your cervix is too small for it to go anywhere. But you can "forget" that you have a tampon in, especially at the end of your period. A tampon that's left in too long can irritate your vagina or even make you sick. (See the discussion of **toxic shock syndrome** in Chapter 6.)

When you're ready to take a tampon out, just pull slowly on the string until it's out. Some tampons can be flushed down the toilet, but some can't be. If you don't know which one yours is, don't flush it. Wrap it in toilet tissue and put it in the garbage.

WHEN YOUR PERIODS STOP

If you haven't had a period by the time you are sixteen, or if you don't have a period for several months, you may have **amenorrhea**. You should see a doctor to find out if there is a problem. Some teenage girls who are very active in sports may not have periods for a while, but not having a period can be a sign that something is wrong.

The egg cells that were in your body when you were born start to run out when you are between forty and sixty years old. There is less of the female hormones that help eggs get ready to meet with sperm. When the eggs are gone, your periods stop. This is called **menopause** or **change of life**. It means you can no longer have babies. Because the hormones are not the same, a woman's body tends to change as she goes into menopause. Her skin gets drier and she may gain or lose weight. Her body tends to change its shape a little.

Some women are sad to stop having menstrual periods because it means an important part of their lives as females has changed, but most are happy to move on to a new stage.

Getting to Know Yourself

Girls are sometimes shy about getting to know their own bodies. There's nothing wrong with getting to know what your body parts are and how they work. It's hard to see your sex organs, even the ones on the outside of the body. You can use a mirror to look at your labia, the clitoris, and the opening of your vagina.

As you get older, you may notice kind of a funny feeling around your vulva when you rub against something or you touch yourself there. Maybe you have an exciting dream and you wake up feeling kind of tingly in your vulva. If you keep touching the clitoris, you may find the feelings getting stronger and stronger. After rubbing or touching for a while, you may have a sudden "swoosh" all over your body.

Getting to know yourself this way is called **masturbation**. Masturbation is normal and even healthy. It's a good way to get to know your body and to find out what kind of touch makes you feel nice. You can masturbate until you feel the "swoosh," but you may not feel it every time you masturbate.

People of all ages masturbate, but not everyone does it. If you masturbate, it's perfectly normal—and if you *don't* masturbate, that's perfectly normal, too.

What's Happening?

Ways your body may be changing:

- Your breasts grow round and bigger.
- Your body is becoming curvy.
- You start having menstrual periods.
- You may start masturbating.

4

What Sex Is All About —and What It Means

Sex is important.

It's what makes new human beings, so it's important to our biology.

It can make us feel good or, sometimes, awful. It's a way to get close to another person—but you or the other person can get hurt as well. So sex is important to our emotions.

Sex or **sexual intercourse** is what brings together a male sperm cell and a female egg cell, but two people can have sex without that happening—and most of the time it doesn't. (Today, science lets people bring together sperm and an egg even *without* sexual intercourse.)

It's simplest to describe sexual intercourse this way: A male's penis is put into a female's vagina. Sperm are pushed out of the penis. They move up the vagina to the Fallopian tubes. They may find an egg there, and one of the sperm may join with the egg to start a baby.

When people talk about sexual intercourse, or just **intercourse,** this is usually what they mean. But there are other ways for people to be sexual with each other, too.

The Way It Works

Getting Close—and Excited

The hormones that make your body change during puberty also make you interested in getting close to another person. You start to get interested in boys, not just as friends, but as something different and special. You find yourself having new feelings. You want to get closer and you may find you want to touch certain boys. You want to hold hands. You think about what it would be like to **kiss** someone.

Teenage boys and girls often tease each other, much more than they did when they were younger. The teasing is sometimes a way to touch without letting anyone know that's what you're trying to do. This kind of teasing is fine, as long as you aren't bothering someone who really doesn't want to play, and as long as it doesn't get mean.

When you are with someone special, you may not just think about holding hands or kissing; you really do it. You may kiss each other on the lips and in other places. You may **French kiss** (also called a tongue kiss), putting your tongues into each other's mouth. (If this sounds gross, then you're not ready to do it—and that's just fine.)

You and the boy you are with may use your hands to touch and rub each other all over your bodies. This used to be called **necking** or **petting** (and your parents may use those words). Today, most young people call it **making out**.

While you are touching and kissing each other, you and the boy you are with are likely to get excited. For a boy, this kind of excitement, called **arousal**, is easy to see: he will start getting an **erection**. In other words, his penis will start getting bigger and hard. It can be embarrassing. Boys can get aroused pretty easily. Even dancing close to another person can sometimes get a boy aroused.

Girls who are aroused may feel themselves getting tingly in the vulva area, or they may feel some liquid coming from their vagina. Their nipples may get hard. Other people may not notice when a girl is aroused.

Boys and girls can get aroused by many things. Sometimes, just reading or thinking about sex can get you aroused. Things that get you aroused are called **erotic**. Erotic reading, movies, or pictures can be done well, or they can be ugly and unhealthy.

Kissing and touching can be very exciting. Many young people kiss and touch and don't do anything more than that. They want to wait until they feel old enough to handle sexual intercourse. Some young people decide to wait to have intercourse until after they are married, because that's what they've learned is right from their religion or their families.

Waiting to have intercourse is a good decision. If you don't feel ready for intercourse, don't let anyone try to talk you into it or, worse, to force you. If you don't want to disappoint your family, or you know you would feel guilty if you had intercourse while you're still young, it's just fine to wait. There are lots of ways to get close to someone, and there's lots of time for you to become **sexually active**.

Think about what you want before you start having boy-friends. Don't fall into sexual activity that doesn't feel right to you.

Beyond Making Out

Making out feels good. It's the body's way of getting ready for intercourse. When a male and female are touching and kissing, the man's penis gets hard so that it can go inside the vagina. At the same time, the woman's vagina becomes wet with **lubrication** from several glands so that a penis can move into it. Kissing and touching to get ready for intercourse are called **foreplay**.

Most men get excited and ready for intercourse quickly, especially when they are young. But sometimes a man may worry about whether he's ready for intercourse, or whether he will be able to make the person he's with feel good. This worry is called **performance anxiety**. Worrying can actually make it difficult for a man to get ready for intercourse. So the more he worries, the more likely he will not be able to have intercourse.

A man's penis going into a woman's vagina is called **vaginal intercourse**. There are a lot of words to describe this, including **coitus** and **copulation**. When two people have intercourse before they're married, it's called **premarital intercourse**. Some people use the word **fornication** to mean intercourse between people who are not married to each other.

During vaginal intercourse, a man puts his erect penis into a woman's vagina. Both of them move so that the penis rubs back and forth against the vaginal walls. Both people get even more excited while they are moving together. They may both have a **climax** or **orgasm**. An orgasm feels like a sudden "whoosh" after all of the excitement during intercourse. A man will almost always experience **ejaculation** during an orgasm, which pushes **semen** filled with sperm into the woman's vagina. Most women have orgasms regularly during sexual intercourse, but some do not and many do not have them all the time. For a woman, an orgasm usually is caused by touching or rubbing against her clitoris.

When people have an orgasm, more hormones are released that make them feel good—and, often, they feel good about the person they just had intercourse with. Intercourse can help people feel connected to each other. That's a good part of a relationship that has **sexual intimacy**. Sometimes people get close to each other because they are having intercourse, even though they don't have much in common. People may tease you that "it's the hormones talking." That teasing can be true.

Other Kinds of Sex

For many people, the word "sex" means vaginal intercourse. There are other kinds of sexual activity:

- **Oral intercourse.** A man's sensitive penis can go into another person's mouth, rather than a vagina. A woman's clitoris can be excited by another person's tongue, rather than during vaginal intercourse. Some teens think that oral intercourse "doesn't count" because you can't make a baby or because a girl's hymen won't be broken by oral intercourse. Oral intercourse can stir up the same complicated feelings as sexual intercourse. Some diseases can be spread by oral intercourse as well.

- **Anal intercourse.** A man's penis may go into another person's anus. The anus is a tighter place than a woman's vagina, which feels good to some men. Anal intercourse can hurt, so both people have to be very careful. You can't get pregnant having anal intercourse. Some diseases can be spread by anal intercourse.

- **Noninsertive sex** or **outercourse.** You can have an orgasm without vaginal, oral, or anal sex. If you and another person touch each other until one or both of you have an orgasm, it can be called outercourse. Sometimes people call it **mutual masturbation**, because what you're really doing is a lot like what you might do if you masturbate. You can't get pregnant from outercourse. If you are having outercourse, you may still spread disease, but it is less likely than with other kinds of sexual activity.

The word **sodomy** is sometimes used to describe any kind of sex other than vaginal intercourse. The word "sodomy" is a negative label: some people use it to say that this kind of sex is bad, but most people don't think of it that way.

When Sex Isn't Good

Sex can be a wonderful thing between two people who care about each other. Because it's so powerful, it can also cause problems. Some diseases are spread through sex. Some people use sex to hurt others.

You Don't Want To

If one person forces another to have sex, it's **rape**. That sounds simple enough, but it's not. You might think of rape as something that happens when someone you don't know, or don't know well, grabs you and forces you to have sex. But what if you are making out with someone you know? You want to stop, but the other person keeps pushing you until you give in. Is that rape? It may be. If you say no and the other person doesn't stop, you have been forced into something bad—and it may be illegal.

When someone you know pushes you into sex when you don't want it, it can be called **date rape** or **acquaintance rape**. Sometimes date rape can be violent, but it isn't always. If you have been drinking or using drugs, you may not be able to say no, but what happens is still rape. A so-called **date rape drug**, dropped into your drink, can make you do things you don't want to.

Sometimes young people are pushed into being sexual with adults they know. It may not be forced, but it is very harmful. You may hear that an adult tried to **molest** someone, or that he or she is a **molester**. The young person may feel that because an adult is trying to do something, the young person can't say no.

You may think of rape as being something that only happens to girls and women, but boys and men can be raped, too.

Protecting Yourself

Make good decisions about your friends and what you do to help protect yourself from sex you don't want:

- Don't put yourself in danger. Don't walk alone at night or in places where there aren't many people around. Don't go to parties or places where you know there will be drinking or drugs. Carry a cell phone. Don't hang out with people who make you uncomfortable.

- Trust your feelings. If you feel nervous about some-one, or about a situation, pay attention. Get away to a place where you feel safe. Call a friend or your family to come get you, if you need to.

- Keep your eye on what you're drinking or eating when in a group. A date rape drug can be slipped into a drink very easily. Stick with water or soda in bottles or cans and open them yourself.

- Make it clear when you are uncomfortable, no matter who is making you feel that way. This can be espe-cially hard to do when an adult—a teacher, a relative, a neighbor—is touching you in ways you don't like. What they are doing is against the law. Tell someone you trust and ask for help.

- Don't date people who make you feel uncomfortable. Someone who tries to kiss or hug you when you don't feel like it is likely to keep pushing.

Statutory Rape

The legal term **statutory rape** is used when one person is older than the other, and the younger person is considered too young to make a decision to have sex, or under **legal age**. The legal age is different in different states. It can be as young as fourteen or as old as eighteen.

The idea is that the older person is taking advantage of the younger person, even if both of them want to have sex. The laws are different. In some states, if the two people are only a couple of years apart in age, it's not statutory rape. In others, it is. The punishment for statutory rape can be very serious, just like the punishment for other kinds of rape.

Unusual Feelings

Sometimes people become aroused by things that are not good. We don't know exactly why. It might be because of things that happened to them when they were children or because of bad experiences they have had.

People who are interested in sex in unusual ways may be called **kinky**. Kinky doesn't always mean bad, just different. People who have sex in ways that are considered bad are called **perverts**. We may call someone a pervert as a joke, but having perverted ideas is actually a serious problem.

In the Family

When brothers, sisters, parents, or other relatives have sex with a young person in the family, it's called **incest**. Almost every culture forbids sex between family members like that.

Children in a family may show each other their sex organs when they are very little. That's a normal part of growing up and figuring out the difference between boys and girls. As you get older, you should be more private (that's why we call them "private parts"). When you start to go into puberty, you should make sure you're not playing games or touching other family members in ways that seem sexual.

If a family member is touching you in ways that feel wrong, tell someone you trust about it. That might mean telling someone outside the family, like a teacher or someone from your church or synagogue.

It's very hard to "tell on" someone in your family. If the person is trying to be sexual with you, he or she is doing something very wrong. You deserve to feel safe in your own home.

Pornography

You can see almost any kind of sex—natural or unnatural—in books, magazines, videos, and even on a lot of Web sites; these things are called **pornography,** and they were created specifically to arouse sexual excitement. If you look at them, you can get the wrong ideas about how people get together. You may find it easier to be sexual with the stuff you see in print and on the computer than it is to date real people. The girls or boys you know probably don't look like the people you see on the computer or in magazines. But the boys and girls you know are real, and they're right here where you can get to know them.

What's Happening?

How sex works:

- Two people get excited together.
- Intercourse may follow excitement.
- Sex is not just one thing.
- Some kinds of sex can be wrong.

5

Falling in Love:
Dating, Love, and So On

You already have a lot of ideas about how they work and what the "rules" are for **love** and sex and relationships. You've watched and learned from your family and friends, most of all, but you also have learned from books, magazines, movies, television, and from other adults, including teachers, coaches, club sponsors, and more.

Humans are social animals, which means we like to live together. That can get complicated—and sometimes it seems like it's complicated even when it isn't. A healthy and loving relationship with another person can make you very happy. Or it can make you confused or unhappy, if things aren't right.

Sex and Morals

There are lots of rules about sex and relationships. Some of them are clear; they come from religious leaders or your parents: Don't have sex unless you're married. Only have certain kinds of sex. Don't have sex with more than one person. Don't have sex with someone of the same gender.

There are also rules that aren't as clear, especially for young people: How old should you be when you have sex the first time? How many people can you have sex with and still be "good"? What kinds of sexual activities are okay and what kinds aren't?

The rules aren't the same for everyone. For example: Some religions say it's wrong for a woman to have sex while she is having her period; other religions don't even talk about that.

The rules, or morals, that come from your family or religious teaching are part of your **morality**. If you follow those rules, you are trying to be **virtuous**. If you don't follow them, you may be considered **immoral**.

Most religions and many families believe that it's not right to have sexual intercourse if you are not married. That's probably not what you see on your favorite television shows, and it's not what you read about in popular magazines, but it's still important to many people.

Some religions talk about a person being **chaste**, which means not having sexual intercourse before **marriage**. It can also mean someone who doesn't date at all, or who doesn't make out or do serious kissing and touching with the people they do date.

A **celibate** person is one who chooses not to have sexual intercourse. Someone can choose to be celibate for a while, or for life. A chaste person is celibate, but someone who was married for years and then lost a **husband** or **wife** may also choose to be celibate at that point.

An important part of living by moral standards—whatever they may be—is making choices that don't hurt other people or yourself. This means not having sex when you don't feel ready for it, or you don't feel good about the other person. It means not trying to push anyone else into having sex or doing sexual things that he or she doesn't want to do. Mostly it means having **self-control**.

That's not always easy, especially for teens. Your hormones are going strong and you may feel that you just can't stop, especially if you are alone with someone you really like. It takes an effort to say "stop," even when you know that's what you need to do. If you don't stop, though, you may feel bad about yourself later. You want to live up to your own set of morals.

Someone who has sex with a lot of people, or who doesn't make good decisions about whom to have sex with, may be called **promiscuous**. Sometimes people get a reputation for being promiscuous when they really aren't. (You may hear that someone is "loose" or "easy.") Girls are more likely than boys to be called promiscuous, because many people expect girls to be more careful about being sexual. That's not fair, but it's something to remember when you make choices about having sexual intercourse.

Think about your rules for dating and sex. Are they the same as your family's rules? How can you try to live up to your rules?

Boys or Girls?

Most of the time, boys want to be sexual with girls, and girls want to be sexual with boys. But most of the time isn't *all* of the time. Some men are attracted to other men, not just as friends but as something closer. Some women are attracted to other women.

People who are attracted to others of the same gender are called **gay** or **homosexual**. (Women who are attracted to other women may also be called **lesbians**.) People who are attracted to the opposite gender are called **straight** or **heterosexual**. **Bisexuals** are attracted to both men and women. Bisexuals can be male or female. The gender you are attracted to is called your **sexual orientation**.

No one knows exactly why some people are attracted to the opposite gender and some are attracted to the same gender. Some researchers believe that you are born gay or straight; others think that your attraction to others happens as you grow up. People don't choose to be gay or straight. It's just the way they feel.

Some people are uncomfortable with homosexuals. They may think it's immoral to be attracted to or to have sex with people of the same gender. They may just not understand how other people can be different from them in the people they love. This kind of fear of homosexuals is called **homophobia**.

Some teens aren't sure about their sexual orientation at first. You might have a crush on a teacher or another student who is the same gender as you. That doesn't mean you are gay. Sometimes it's hard to tell the difference between admiring and liking someone as a friend and having feelings for them. You may start **dating** people of the opposite gender and discover after a while that you are really more attracted to people of your own gender. Some young people need to explore their feelings for a while. Others know exactly how they feel about dating and sexuality as soon as they start adolescence. Both of these are perfectly normal.

If you are confused about whether you're straight or gay, talk to someone you trust about your feelings. Ask for ideas about books or videos that can help you understand what it means.

Falling in Like

When you're born, you don't know what love is; you just know that those around you—your mother and father, brothers and sisters, daycare teachers and whoever else—give you food when you're hungry, hold you, rock you, and make funny noises at you. It's all kind of a big blur of others making sure you're comfortable.

Pretty quickly, you start to notice that the big blur is separate people. You start to get attached to them. You feel good when you hear your mother's voice and are held in her warm arms. You like the deeper voices you hear from your father and other men. Maybe you have a sister who coos at you and makes you laugh. All of these good feelings start to be something that we call love.

You *learn* to love other people. You hear your mother and father and others telling you they love you, especially when they're hugging you and kissing you, so you start to connect that word "love" with being close to other people who care for you.

That kind of feeling or **affection** for your family and friends is different from the **romantic love** you will feel one day for someone you want to be with. But it's hard to fall in love if you don't know how to be close to other people already.

Sometimes even very small children have friends that are "special" to them. They really want to play with that particular toddler or preschooler. This doesn't have anything to do with sex or hormones. It's just wanting to spend time with someone they feel particularly close to. Those feelings also are part of learning to love a partner someday.

Did you have a "special friend" when you were little? Try to remember why you liked that other child and wanted to be close to him or her.

When you go into adolescence, and your hormones are giving you some new feelings, the whole idea of love and affection starts to be different. A special friend may not just be someone you like to talk to and play with, but someone you want to be close to in other ways. You may imagine, or **fantasize**, how you can show your affection. Sometimes teens feel attached to someone they haven't even met, like a movie star, musician, or athlete. That's normal—and can be kind of fun—as long as it doesn't go too far. Don't spend more time thinking about your fantasies than you spend with real people.

Thinking about the person—or people—you want to get close to can make you change some things in your life. You start to pay attention to how you look and dress, hoping that the boy or girl you're interested in will notice you. You find excuses to hang out around them. You want more than friendship, you want a little **romance**.

Dating

Teens who are interested in romance and getting close often start by hanging out in groups. You and a few of your friends meet another small group, and you all go to a movie or get a pizza. Everyone is laughing and teasing each other, but the people who like each other in a special way kind of manage to sit next to each other or even hold hands in the middle of the group.

Parents may like it if you stick to groups, because they think you can't get too sexual as long as there are other people around. That's not necessarily true, but being in a group can help you avoid doing anything you don't feel you're ready for. It's also a good way to get to know someone without a lot of pressure.

At some point, you may want to be with someone when it's just the two of you. The age when you do this depends on what you feel ready for—and what your family's rules are. Some families don't allow dating until age fifteen or sixteen or even eighteen. It's a teen's job to think these rules are unfair, but your family sets them for good reasons.

There is a lot of pressure on teens to be sexy and sexual, even when they're not comfortable with it. If your family has a rule against dating, it gives you a good excuse to say no to getting sexual too soon.

But I'm ready! you think. Physically you may be, especially if you are a girl. Girls are ready to have sex—and make babies—not long after starting to menstruate.

Having a body that is ready is not the same thing as having a brain and feelings and a life ready for serious dating. The hardest thing about being a teen is giving yourself time to get ready for more adult things in life, when everything—from your hormones to the television shows you watch to your friends—is telling you that you can do adult things right this minute.

When Is It Dating?

When you are dating someone, it's more than just great friendship. You feel like you want to be close to him. You may be nervous about what he thinks of you. It feels good to hold hands, or to put your arm around the other person. You are thinking about him a lot. When you go out, it doesn't matter that much if you do anything special—it's special just to be together.

Dating doesn't mean having sex. Some people who date have sex. Some just kiss and hug. Dating is spending time together, caring about each other and sharing feelings. When you're dating someone, you may become **intimate**, which means getting very close. (Sometimes people use the word "intimate" to mean having sex, but it means much more than just that.) Getting that close is exciting and sometimes a little scary. If you care a lot about someone else, that person can hurt your feelings

If you are infatuated with someone else, you make that person the center of your world, which is not healthy. You can be infatuated with someone you're dating, calling the person all the time, trying to spend all of your free time with her or him, thinking and talking about the person until your friends are tired of it. You can also be infatuated with someone you barely know—or maybe don't know at all. Your **infatuation** can make you sad or angry, because you never seem to get enough of the other person's attention or time.

People who are infatuated may think that they have a great **passion**—superstrong feelings of love. Infatuation is more about your feelings than those of the person you're infatuated with. Caring for someone means sharing, not just thinking about how someone else makes you feel. People—young people and those who have been dating for many years—may think that if they are **jealous** and anxious about the person they're dating, it shows they really care.

Dating shouldn't be that serious. Dating should be fun.

Dating Tips for Teens

- Know your "rules" for dating. Before you start dating, think about what your values are and how you want to live up to them. Do you want to wait to have sex? Are you uncomfortable with too much making out? What do you want to do if your date is drinking or using drugs? Your values come from what your parents have taught you, your religion, and what you know about yourself. Have a little talk with yourself about what you want so that you won't be trying to figure things out while you're in the middle of a date.

- Be part of a group. You probably will start dating someone you already know from school or an activity. That makes a lot of sense. The two of you will have something in common and you may already know each other. It's easier to ask someone out on a date—or to be asked out—if it's already clear that the two of you like each other as friends. If your first dates are with the group, it can feel pretty comfortable.

- Check your feelings about the other person. What do you like about him? Are there things you don't like? You can get caught up dating someone you don't like that much, or don't have much in common with, just because he is popular or very attractive. (You might also miss out on dating someone you like just because he is not as popular as you want.) Don't date someone just because you think that person's popularity will somehow rub off on you.

- Be yourself. Yes, you want to look your best and you want your date to like you; that's part of the fun of dating. But if you are always worrying about what you say and do, then maybe this isn't the right person to date. Make sure your date knows the real you—and likes that person, not someone you're trying to be.

- Have a safety plan. Bad things can happen, no matter how well you think you know the person you're dating. Take a cell phone with you. Make sure your family knows where you will be and when you will be home. Carry a little extra money so that you can call a cab if you need to. Don't end up in a bad situation with no way to get out of it.

- Don't do anything that makes you uncomfortable. Trust your feelings, even—especially—if your date is making fun of them. If you feel like something is wrong, chances are you're right. Don't drink if you think it's a bad idea. Don't go places you feel unsafe. Don't stay with a person or people you don't feel good about.

- Stay in your own age group. Especially when you are a teen, it's best to date people around your same age. Older boys and girls can seem smart and experienced and sexy, but they may be a little too experienced for you. They may push you to do things you're just not ready for (and yes, this is true for both boys and girls). Younger boys and girls may look at *you* as the smart, experienced, sexy one—and you can take advantage of them without realizing you're doing it.

- Learn about the person you're with. Finding out who the person you're dating really is can be part of the fun. Ask questions. Encourage him to talk about his likes and dislikes, hobbies, friends, family, and almost anything else you can think of. You may be charmed by his super biceps, but you need to know the whole person.

- Be kind. You know how easily your feelings can be hurt. The person you are dating—or want to date— probably feels the same way. The old-fashioned advice to just be nice goes a long way. Don't say nasty things to the other person—or about the other person. Be there when you say you're going to be there. Don't sulk or act angry, especially when the person you're with doesn't have anything to do with why you're angry. If you don't want to date someone, or you want to stop dating that person, try to explain why in a kind way.

- Talk with an adult you trust. You have a lot of questions when you're dating. Your friends will have plenty of answers, but most of them are in about the same place you are and their answers may not be the right ones for you. If you have a good relationship with your parents or guardian and can talk to them comfortably about dating, trust them with your questions. If you feel uncomfortable talking with them about dating and sexuality, try to find another adult you can confide in safely.

- Don't worry if you *aren't* dating. Not everyone dates in junior high and high school. Some teens aren't ready—or even interested. Others are interested, but it just doesn't happen for them. You may ask yourself, "What's wrong with me?" The answer is: Probably nothing. Some people are just slower to get into dating. If you think there might be something about you that is keeping people away, talk to a few people you trust—adults and other teens—and ask them to be honest with you.

Remember: Dating is practice for being with another person in a relationship. When you practice anything, you make mistakes—and learn from them.

Think about your values or "rules" for dating and write them down as a reminder of your own values.

When Dating Doesn't Feel Good

Don't let yourself be treated badly. When you really like someone, you may not see that he is not being nice to you. You may start to think that it's all your fault; you're just not good enough. No matter what you've done—or think you've done—you should never be treated badly by the person you're dating. Never.

You and the person you're dating should be equals. You like and respect each other—and you treat each other that way. If one person is trying to control the other, it can become an **abusive relationship**. An abusive relationship can be violent, but it doesn't have to be. You can be hurt by someone who says and does things to make you feel bad, even if he never touches you.

If you start to feel bad about yourself while dating someone, you may be in an abusive relationship. Ask yourself whether your partner:

- Says things like, "If you love me, you will . . ." This is a way he pushes you to do what he wants—not what you want.

- Keeps you away from your friends and family. The other person wants you all to himself. That may sound very romantic at first. It's not. It's a way for the abusive person to take over your life. Without your friends and family, you don't have people who can help you see the truth about the relationship.

- Tells you what's wrong with you all the time. An abusive person will try to make you feel bad about yourself. It may seem like joking or teasing at first. You feel silly getting upset. Over time, you just keep trying to please him, but you never can.

- Accuses you of being with other people. Even if you never look at anyone else, an abusive person says you're flirting or trying to date someone else. The more you try to prove you aren't, the more control the abusive person has over you.

- Checks up on you all the time. He calls you, e-mails you, hangs around outside your house. You're told that you can't be trusted.

- Pushes you to do things you don't want to do. An abusive person may want you to lie to your family, drink alcohol, use drugs, be more sexual, behave in ways that just aren't you. You give in because you think you

love him, or because you don't want to cause a fight,
but you don't like yourself for caving.

In an abusive relationship, the abusive person often says or
does something hurtful, then apologizes and promises never to do
it again—and then does it again and again.

Both boys and girls can be abusive. Girls are not as likely to
be physically abusive—but it can happen.

You may need help getting out of an abusive relationship.
Abusive people can be worse when someone decides to break it
off. When you tell someone you're not going to see him anymore,
get some support from friends and family. Don't have that talk
when you are alone with the abusive person.

Making a Commitment

Relationships in every part of the world started out a long, long
time ago based on creating and raising children. It's more complicated today: Some people never have children, some have children
but don't live with the other parent. Some people live with others
of the same sex.

When we talk about a **traditional family**, we mean a family
with a **husband**, a **wife**, and children. The husband and wife are
spouses, or **mates**, who pledge to live together by getting married.

Marriage is the official legal way that two people commit
to living together and, maybe, starting a family. In most of the
world, marriage is between one man and one woman, but that's
not the only kind of marriage. Some religions and countries allow
a man to have more than one wife, which is called **polygamy**.

For most people, getting married means making a commit-
ment to be sexual only with your spouse. This is called **monogamy**. When married people have sex with someone other than
their spouse, it's called **adultery**.

In America, people usually choose their own spouses. They may date several people before deciding that one of them is someone they want to marry. Some other cultures believe in **arranged marriage**, one in which your family chooses a spouse for you. In those cultures, you may not meet your husband or wife until your wedding day, or just before it.

There are happy—and unhappy—marriages, whether they have been arranged by families or the two spouses have chosen each other. What's important in the long run is how people treat each other.

What's Happening?

How dating works:

- You develop values and morals.
- You learn to care about others.
- You spend time with someone special.
- You make sure you're treated well.

6

Take Care of Your Body —It's the Only One You Have

Adolescents get colds and the flu, just like adults and little kids. They sprain ankles and get bruises just like people who are older and younger. Some illnesses and health concerns, however, are particularly important for teens to understand. Adolescents are learning about sex—so it's important they also learn there are illnesses that can be passed from one person to another during sex.

Eating Right

You may be tired of your parents, teachers, and coaches telling you things like "eat the right foods, get plenty of sleep, exercise." What they're saying is true for everyone, no matter what age, but it's especially important during your adolescent years, when your body is changing. Taking care of your body now can help you stay healthy as you get older.

When you hang out with your friends, you want to have pizza, hamburgers, tacos, ice cream, chicken wings . . . almost everything that's fried or loaded with sugar and **calories**. Let's face it: all of those things taste great.

You sleep late in the morning, so you skip breakfast. A bag of chips and a soda at lunch and then you get home so late that your family has already eaten dinner, so you grab something out of the freezer and nuke it in the microwave for dinner.

These kinds of eating habits do bad things to your body. You're still growing and changing, and your body needs the right kind of energy to handle that. If you eat healthy foods most of the time, you can splurge on pizza and burgers once in a while when you go out with friends.

A Healthy Diet

There are hundreds of diet books around. They recommend everything from eating lots of grapefruit to eating everything you want except breads, rice, and other **carbohydrates**. The basic healthy diet is pretty simple, though.

The United States Department of Agriculture developed a food pyramid decades ago, before your parents were born. It's been updated by the Harvard School of Public Health, but it still concentrates on the same things: eat lots of fresh fruits and vegetables and less meat—especially red meat like beef; include more **whole grains**; cut back on salt and sugar; and make sure the portion sizes you eat are reasonable.

Don't Skip Meals

Missing meals tends to make you eat the wrong food at the wrong time. Make sure you make time for breakfast every morning—even if you're grabbing a healthy breakfast bar and some juice or milk before you run out the door.

Drink Right

Soda gives you a lot of sugar you just don't need, but many young people just love it. Switch to diet soda or, better, water.

There are lots of flavored waters with no calories that are actually good for you.

Ahh, Sleep

You still need eight to nine hours of sleep each night, but your body may not want to let you fall asleep until 11 at night or later. If you have to wake up at 6 the next morning, you're not going to get the sleep you need. When you don't get enough sleep at night:

- You may be sleepy during the day. Have you ever fallen asleep at your desk during class?
- You're more likely to have an accident while driving.
- You may not do as well in school, even if you manage to stay awake during class.
- You may feel sad or angry. When you don't have enough sleep, it's harder to control your moods.
- You are more likely to smoke or use alcohol or drugs.
- Teens who take part in school activities, jobs, and other activities—and who don't have time to get the sleep they need—are more likely to feel the effects of losing sleep.

It may seem like your life doesn't give you enough time to sleep when you need to, and that's a real problem. Try to make some time:

- Get yourself into bed at a reasonable hour, turn out the lights, put on some soft music, and let yourself drift off to sleep. A glass of milk and a cookie or graham cracker before you go to bed sometimes helps you fall asleep.

- Look at the activities you're involved in and see if there are some you can give up or put off until another time.
- Leave yourself time to catch up a little on weekends. This isn't as good as getting enough sleep every night, but it helps. Sleep late, take a nap—and tell your family you really need it!

Get Moving

When your parents or grandparents were going to school, they probably walked or biked every day. They may have had chores to do that kept them outside and active. Very few people had computers, and there weren't hundreds of cable channels. They got exercise almost without trying.

Teens today are less likely to get out and get going. With video games, computers, dozens of television programs and movies to watch (even on your phone), it's easy to spend most of a day hanging out on the couch.

If you're on a team or involved in sports in some way, your coach is probably giving you a regular exercise program, besides sports practice, which is great. Even kids on teams need to exercise during the off-season, or to work some muscles that are different from those needed for their particular sport.

Teens who exercise are less likely to smoke or use drugs and alcohol and more likely to sleep well, get good grades, and feel good about themselves.

Getting exercise doesn't have to be complicated: walking, running, and biking are good overall exericse for you, and easy to do. The main thing is to turn off the television or the computer and get yourself off the couch and out of the house.

Love Your Body

It's normal to think a lot about how you look, especially when it seems like your body is changing almost every day. Girls and boys think about how they look to other people, and whether they are pretty or handsome—or not.

There's a difference between normal interest in how you look and an unhealthy interest. The way you think about yourself is your **body image**. A healthy body image means accepting your own body for what it is. That doesn't mean you think you look perfect, just that you're okay with yourself. An unhealthy body image means you don't like the way you look. It probably has nothing to do with how others see you; it's just that when you look in the mirror, you see something you don't like. Other people may think you're beautiful, but you don't like yourself. This can be a serious problem, because an unhealthy body image can lead to your treating yourself badly.

Certain kinds of **eating disorders** are more likely to show up during the teen years than later—although they can happen at any time. These eating disorders can happen because of an unhealthy body image, or they can start for other reasons but have an unhealthy body image as part of what they do to you.

A Need to Stay Thin

People with **anorexia nervosa** (which is sometimes just called anorexia) think they are too fat, no matter how thin they really are. They try to avoid eating as much as they can. They may do a number of different things to try to lose weight:

- Diet pills or other drugs
- Refusing to eat in front of other people

- Pushing food around a plate, but not eating it
- Eating only tiny amounts of food, like one lettuce leaf for a salad

Someone with anorexia can actually starve to death. The body starts to have a number of bad symptoms when it doesn't get enough food, from creaking bones to dry skin to organs shutting down. Having anorexia as a teen can cause problems later in life, even if you get over it.

Girls are much more likely to develop anorexia than boys, although boys can have problems, too. Girls who are in sports or other activities, like ballet, where staying thin is emphasized, are at greater risk of developing anorexia.

Not everyone who goes on a diet is going to be anorexic. In fact, only a tiny number of people are. But it is a serious illness that can threaten your life. If you think you (or a friend) might have a bad relationship with food, tell an adult you trust.

Bulimia nervosa or bulimia is like anorexia, except that the person who has it does eat—and sometimes eats a lot—and then does things to get the food out of the body before it's digested. People with bulimia may make themselves throw up or may use drugs to **purge** food from their bodies.

Some people do **binge eating**—eating a lot of food at once— and then force themselves to throw up or get rid of the food another way so that they stay thin.

Another way to try to stay thin is **compulsive exercising**. Some people eat normal meals (or they binge), but instead of trying to throw up, they force themselves to exercise. Regular exercise is good for you, but if you are exercising all the time, so much that you aren't paying attention to friends or schoolwork or other activities, it becomes a problem.

A person with anorexia has an unhealthy body image and may do compulsive exercise, as well as refusing to eat.

Can't Stop Eating?

Compulsive overeating or **food addiction** can be a way to try to feel better, even though it only makes you feel worse. Compulsive eaters just can't push food away. When they're sad, they eat—and they eat a lot. When they're angry, they eat. As they gain weight, they like themselves less and less, but they can't stop eating. Some compulsive eaters also have bulimia, so they may not gain a great deal of weight. Many do not also have bulimia, however.

Compulsive overeating doesn't mean you enjoy your food—most compulsive eaters do not. They eat because they feel bad. They've learned to eat when something is bothering them, thinking it will make them feel better. Instead, they often feel embarrassed, ashamed, and sad.

Obesity

Obesity means that your body has too much fat. That will show on the outside, but the real danger is on the inside, where the extra fat and weight make you more likely to develop heart disease, some kinds of cancer, **diabetes**, and many other illnesses.

Obesity is a real problem in the United States. Experts say that almost 18 percent of young people from twelve to nineteen years old are obese. Obese young people are more likely to be obese as adults—and are more likely to have health problems because of their weight.

An eating disorder, like compulsive overeating, can cause obesity, but not everyone who is obese has an eating disorder. If you eat a lot because you just enjoy the food, you may not have an eating disorder—but you can be unhealthy because you become obese.

Just for Females

The female body is so complex that there is a kind of doctor that specializes in taking care of women, the **gynecologist**. **Gynecology** deals with the diseases and care of women's sexual organs.

You may have had the same doctor since you were a baby, giving you shots and taking care of you when you got a cold. As you go into adolescence, it may be time to see a gynecologist for your first **gynecological exam**. Doctors recommend that girls have their first exam between the ages of thirteen and fifteen, around the time they are getting their first period.

At the first exam, the gynecologist may just talk to you about how things are going. Girls often worry about having someone else look at them "down there," especially if the doctor is a man, but the first thing the doctor wants to do is understand how you are feeling and what's happening with your body.

Questions the doctor may ask include:

- When did you start menstruating?
- When was your last period?
- Are you having any problems with your period?
- Are you sexually active?
- Are you using **birth control**?

Pelvic Exam

At some point, you will have a **pelvic exam**. This may not be for several years after your first visit. The pelvic exam is to check your sex organs to see if there are any health problems. Women have pelvic exams regularly to make sure nothing has changed.

During a pelvic exam, you will be lying on an examining table, undressed from the waist down, with a sheet covering you. You will lie back on the table and put your feet in stirrups, which hold your legs apart so the doctor can examine your vaginal area. If the doctor needs to look inside the vagina, he or she will use a **speculum**. This tool fits into your vagina and then opens slightly so that the doctor can see better. It can feel strange, but it's only for a minute and it won't hurt you.

Pap Test

One of the regular tests a gynecologist does for women is the **Pap test** or **Pap smear**. This test checks for cervical cancer. It only takes minutes, but it can save lives. Gynecologists recommend that you have your first Pap smear when you are twenty-one, or within three years of becoming sexually active. For the Pap smear, the doctor opens the lips of your vagina using a speculum, then uses a long swab (like a Q-tip) to take a sample of cells from the outer opening of the cervix. That mucus is sent to a lab and tested for cancer.

Breast Exam

Although teens don't usually develop breast cancer, your gynecologist will do a breast exam when you come for a regular physical exam and should teach you how to do the **breast self-examination (BSE)** by yourself. The doctor will gently press around your breast in circles, checking for lumps that feel unusual.

If your doctor doesn't show you how to examine your own breasts, ask. You can also pick up a pamphlet at the gynecologist's office or go online to find instructions for the exam.

Itching and Burning

A number of things can cause itching and burning in the vulva and vaginal area. Some are serious, some are not. This kind of itching and burning is called **vaginitis**.

One kind of vaginitis is a **yeast infection**, which is actually caused by a fungus. This fungus is always in your vagina, but when something changes, it can grow too quickly. You can get a yeast infection from taking antibiotics for another illness or even from wearing panties or jeans that are too tight. The fungus grows more when the area around the vagina is kept very moist.

If you have a yeast infection, you will feel itching and soreness and you may see discharge that looks kind of like cottage cheese. A yeast infection does not have a bad smell.

There are medicines you can buy without a prescription to treat a yeast infection, but it's good to check with a doctor first. You may think you have a yeast infection, but it can be something else.

Urinary Infection

If you feel pain when you urinate, you may have a **urinary tract infection**, or **UTI**. Both men and women can get urinary tract infections, but women are much more likely to. If you have a urinary tract infection, you need to be treated by a doctor—especially if you feel pain in your abdomen or you see blood in your urine.

Some young women get urinary tract infections often; others rarely or never get one. You can help reduce your risk of a urinary tract infection by:

- Drinking plenty of liquids. Water is best, but many women say cranberry juice really helps them.
- Wiping from front to back. When you have a bowel movement, wipe yourself from the front to the back so that you don't get any feces in the vaginal area.
- Urinating when you need to. Don't try to "hold it."
- Avoiding powders, sprays, or other products in your genital area. The chemicals and perfumes can irritate.

Toxic Shock Syndrome

If you don't change your tampon often enough, you can develop **toxic shock syndrome**, or **TSS**. This was a serious problem in the late 1970s, because of a kind of superabsorbent tampon that was widely in use at the time. Today, TSS is rare, but it can still happen.

Toxic shock syndrome develops when bacteria on the tampon inside your body multiply while the tampon is in your body. The bacteria then enter the bloodstream and infect your whole body. The illness causes anything from a skin rash to organ failure and death.

Although you can get toxic shock syndrome even if you don't use tampons—and men, small children, and women who aren't having their period can get it, too—menstruating women are most likely to get it. Signs of toxic shock syndrome are:

- Fever higher than 102 degrees
- A rash like sunburn all over the body
- Vomiting and diarrhea
- Feeling weak, with aching muscles
- Headaches
- Being confused and not knowing where you are

To avoid getting toxic shock syndrome, you can use sanitary pads instead of tampons. If you use tampons, change them often and use ones that are less absorbent. Try using tampons for only part of your period and sanitary pads the rest of the time.

Pelvic Inflammatory Disease

Pelvic inflammatory disease (PID) is an infection of the organs in your pelvic area: the uterus, Fallopian tubes, ovaries, cervix, and vagina. It's caused by bacteria that get into the pelvic area through the vagina, usually through sexual intercourse. Using a douche and some kinds of birth control also can cause PID.

You can have pelvic inflammatory disease and not know it. That's bad because PID can cause very serious problems, including making it impossible for you to get pregnant and have children. Symptoms you might have include:

- Fever
- Smelly vaginal discharge
- Pain when you urinate
- Irregular periods
- Pain in the stomach area

If you are sexually active and you have these symptoms, see a doctor right away. PID can spread to your organs quickly.

Ovarian Cysts

Some women develop a bulge of fluid (called an **ovarian cyst**) in one or both ovaries. Most of these cysts are benign, or harmless, but they can cause pain or bleeding. They can grow in your body at any age, but usually they only happen while you are menstruating.

If you have a cyst, you might have:

- An ache in your lower abdomen, or sharp pains every once in a while
- Pain in your abdomen right before or after your period
- Irregular periods or spotting
- Pains in your ribs
- Lumps you can feel in your abdomen
- Problems urinating or having bowel movements
- A tired feeling
- A heavy, full feeling in your abdomen

Cysts can be very small, like the size of a pea, or as big as a melon. Depending on the size and how you're feeling, your doctor may just watch the cyst to see what happens or take it out in surgery.

Osteoporosis

Osteoporosis is a disease that makes your bones brittle and weaker, so they break more easily. Osteoporosis shows up when you are older, usually after you have gone through menopause, but things you do as a teen and young woman can reduce your chances of having osteoporosis later.

Good diet and regular exercise, starting as early as you can, and continuing throughout your life, can help you be a healthier woman when you are past menopause. Other things you can do include drinking milk, not smoking, and being careful with alcohol.

Female Athletic Syndrome or Female Athlete Triad

If you play sports very hard, especially a sport like long-distance running, you can develop **female athletic syndrome** or **female athlete triad**. This is really a combination of three different symptoms: an eating disorder, bone problems that can lead to early osteoporosis, and problems with menstruation.

Sexually Transmitted Diseases

Some diseases can be spread, or **transmitted**, by sexual intercourse. The damp, warm area around a person's sex organs is a perfect place for different kinds of bacteria and viruses to grow and spread.

Diseases that are spread mostly through sexual activity are called **sexually transmitted diseases,** or **STDs.** You may also hear them called **venereal diseases.** Some STDs are annoying but will not hurt you. Some are serious and can make you very sick, or make it impossible for you to have children when you want to. Not being able to make eggs or sperm is called **sterility.** People can be sterile for various reasons, not only because of venereal disease.

Your Behavior

Anyone who is sexually active can get an STD. You may be very careful, but you don't always know everything about the people you are having sex with. **Safe behavior** or **preventive behavior** means doing things to make it less likely you will get an STD. Safe behavior involves, among other things:

- Knowing as much as you can about the sexual history of the people you are involved with.
- Using protection, like **condoms,** to protect you from the spread of bacteria or viruses.
- Having outercourse or noninsertive sex.

People sometimes talk about having **safe sex,** or **safer sex.** This means using protection, like condoms, or having sex that does not involve **penetration.**

Risky behavior is doing things that can make it more likely you will get an STD, such as having sex with a number of people—including people you don't know well—or not using any kind of protection during sex.

Common STDs

There are a number of STDs, some serious and some not, that doctors see frequently.

CHLAMYDIA

Chlamydia is a common STD that affects both men and women. Often there are no symptoms of chlamydia. If you have chlamydia and don't get it taken care of, it can lead to more serious problems. Chlamydia can hurt the Fallopian tubes and cause sterility.

Symptoms for women can be discharge or irritation of the vaginal area, pain in the lower abdomen, or pain when urinating.

PUBIC LICE

Pubic lice are little bugs that get into your pubic hair. They may be called **crabs** or **crab lice** because they look like tiny crabs. They are usually spread from one person to another during sexual activity, while the two bodies are close together. But you can also get pubic lice from towels, bedding, and even another person's clothes.

If you have pubic lice, you may have itching in your pubic area, especially at night. Scratching the area that itches can cause infection and make it worse.

Treating pubic lice is not difficult. There are **prescription drugs** and other treatments to kill them. You should clean any clothing or bedding you used while you had lice.

GENITAL HERPES

About one of every four women and one of every eight men have had a **genital herpes** infection. Genital herpes is a virus that is spread during sexual contact. Genital herpes can cause painful sores on your genitals, which appear and then go away. Some people have herpes but don't know it. Others may have symptoms that include sores, feeling achy, and fever.

If a woman has a breakout of genital herpes while giving birth, the baby can be harmed.

There is no cure for genital herpes. Once you have it, you will have it for the rest of your life—although you may have very few outbreaks. Most people live with it without serious problems, but it is an STD and you should be very careful both about avoiding getting herpes and about spreading it.

Don't have sex if you are having an outbreak of sores, and don't have sex with anyone else who is having an outbreak. Protection (such as condoms) can help prevent the spread of herpes.

HUMAN PAPILLOMAVIRUS

The **human papillomavirus** or **HPV** is spread through sexual intercourse. Both men and women can get HPV, but the problems for women are much more serious—and they take a long time to develop. Most people who get HPV don't get sick in any way, although some get warts in their genital areas. About half of the men and women in the United States who are sexually active will have HPV at some time during their lives, but most will never know it.

Some kinds of HPV—not the same kinds that cause warts— can cause cervical cancer and other kinds of cancers in the genital area years after you are infected. Cervical cancer doesn't usually have symptoms until it has grown and is serious.

The new **human papillomavirus vaccine** can prevent the kinds of HPV that cause cancer and warts. Doctors recommend that girls get the vaccine (three shots over six months) when they are eleven or twelve years old. They also recommend that you have it if you are thirteen to twenty-six years old and have not been vaccinated.

GENITAL WARTS

Genital warts are caused by the human papillomavirus. They can show up on the penis and around the anus, or around the vagina. The warts can be very tiny or they can be in big groups.

Sometimes genital warts disappear without any medical treatment. Doctors have several different ways to take care of genital warts, from medicated creams to laser surgery.

Even if the warts are gone, you still have HPV. The warts can come back later.

TRICHOMONIASIS

Trichomoniasis is caused by a parasite. It is common in young women, although men get it, too. The symptoms of trichomoniasis for women are a smelly vaginal discharge, as well as itching and irritation around the genitals. Men usually don't have any symptoms—and men almost always get trichomoniasis by having sex with a woman who has it.

A doctor will prescribe drugs that can cure trichomoniasis. If you don't get treated, you will keep on spreading trichomoniasis to anyone you have sex with.

GONORRHEA

Gonorrhea is a common STD, caused by the **gonococcus** bacteria. It can cause serious problems, including sterility, especially in women, but it almost always can be cured with antibiotics.

A woman with gonorrhea may have vaginal discharge, trouble urinating, and spotting between periods. A man may have trouble urinating and may have discharge from the penis.

NONGONOCOCCAL URETHRITIS

Nongonococcal urethritis is an infection of the urethra that is not caused by gonorrhea. It can be caused by an injury or an infection, usually an STD. It can usually be treated with antibiotics.

SYPHILIS

Syphilis is caused by bacteria. It is an extremely serious STD, but luckily it can be cured with antibiotics if it's caught early.

Syphilis starts with a sore, called a **chancre**, at the spot where syphilis first got into the body. Usually this will be on the penis or the vulva. The sore will heal, but syphilis is still in your body. Weeks later, you may break out in a rash and have other symptoms, like swollen glands, a sore throat, aching muscles, and an overall tired feeling.

These symptoms will go away, but syphilis stays in your body and can come back years later—even twenty years later—and damage your organs. In its last stage, syphilis can cause blindness, paralysis, and even death.

If you have a sore in your genital area, and you are sexually active, have it checked by a doctor. A doctor will look at cells from the sore or chancre or take a blood sample to see if there are any **spirochetes**, the bacteria that cause syphilis.

HEPATITIS

There are several kinds of **hepatitis**, which is an inflammation of the liver. Hepatitis A is transmitted through the feces of people who are infected. Often, this happens when you eat food that has been made by someone who didn't wash his or her hands properly after using the bathroom. You can get very ill from hepatitis A, but once you've had it, you will be protected from getting it again.

Hepatitis B and hepatitis C are both spread through sexual activity. They can cause serious damage to your liver, or even death.

Symptoms of hepatitis include:

- Fever
- Feeling sick to your stomach
- No appetite
- Pain on the upper right side of the abdomen
- Dark urine
- Light-colored bowel movements
- Yellow skin and eyes

There is no sure cure for hepatitis B and C, but they can sometimes be treated with medicine.

AIDS (ACQUIRED IMMUNODEFICIENCY SYNDROME)

The most serious STD is **acquired immunodeficiency syndrome** or **AIDS**. Although doctors are developing drugs to treat it, it can't be cured and if it's not treated, it almost always leads to death.

AIDS is caused by the **human immunodeficiency virus (HIV)**, which is spread through sexual contact or through blood contact. Normally, your body's **immune system** makes **antibodies** that fight off any illness or infection. HIV affects the immune system, so diseases can make you very ill, very quickly.

HIV also destroys white blood cells, or **T-cells,** which also makes you more likely to become sick from different diseases.

Once you have HIV, you are likely to develop AIDS. You have AIDS when the number of T-cells in your body has dropped to a very low level and you have started to develop certain kinds of diseases. Drug treatment can make it take longer for an HIV infection to become AIDS, but it doesn't cure HIV and the drug treatment is very expensive.

Because AIDS is so serious, it's important to be very careful about who you have sexual contact with. There is no second chance with AIDS.

Dangerous Activities

"Oh, don't worry, I'll be okay," you tell your parents. And you mean it. Teens think that nothing bad can happen to them. It's a great feeling, but it just isn't true. You're starting to explore the world in new ways, and sometimes that leads you into dangerous activities or habits.

Consuming Alcohol

Alcohol is everywhere. You see it on television and in movies; your parents may drink wine or beer or cocktails. It looks like alcohol is the way to have fun. It's illegal for anyone under twenty-one to drink, but somehow kids you know are finding ways to get alcohol and to drink it. If you say no, will you be a party pooper?

Teens who drink:

- Are more likely to be in accidents.
- Do worse in school.
- Are more likely to have unsafe sex.
- Are more likely to hurt themselves.

When you drink too much, you don't make good decisions about what you're doing. You may end up in sexual situations you don't like—or that are even dangerous.

Alcoholism is when you don't just like alcohol, you can't do without it. You can start developing alcoholism when you are young. Experts estimate that more than three million teens are alcoholics and millions more can't handle their drinking.

Some people don't drink all the time, but when they do drink, they drink a lot. This **binge drinking** can kill you. Too much alcohol in your blood can lead to **alcohol poisoning**, which can cause death.

Signs of alcohol poisoning are:

- Throwing up
- Very slow breathing
- Ten seconds or more between breaths
- Low body temperature
- Confusion or a complete blackout

If someone has alcohol poisoning, you can't get the person over it with coffee or a cold shower. He or she needs to get to a doctor right away. Don't let someone "sleep it off" if he or she has symptoms of alcohol poisoning after binge drinking. A person with alcohol poisoning may choke or stop breathing and die while unconscious.

Taking Drugs

There are many kinds of drugs around, and teens in most parts of the United States can find them if they want to. All of them can hurt you, but some are very dangerous.

Teens take drugs because they think drugs will make them seem more adult, or they like the feeling of being high. Some drugs can cause **addiction,** meaning that once you start taking them, you can't do without them. You need to keep taking the drugs or your body will start to feel bad. Sometimes you need to take more and more of a drug in order to get the feeling you want.

Drugs are dangerous at any age, but while your body is still growing and developing, they can cause permanent problems.

A **drug overdose,** when you take too much of a drug, can kill you. Illegal drugs are extremely powerful.

It's not just illegal drugs that can cause problems. Some prescription drugs that are meant to be used for an illness—yours or someone else's—can cause addiction. And some things you can buy in a drugstore without a prescription can become dangerous drugs if you take too much of them.

Smoking

Why would you want to do something that makes your breath and your clothes smell bad, that stains your teeth, and makes you feel tired?

You may think that smoking cigarettes makes you look older and more sophisticated. After all, some of your favorite movie stars and music idols smoke.

Smoking is addictive, which means that once you start, it's very hard to stop. Teens who smoke often wish many years later that they'd never started.

Cigarette smoking can lead to cancer, heart disease, and lung disease. It may take years for anything like that to develop, but even now you can make yourself sick with cigarettes. You're even likely to get more colds.

Driving

Nearly 40 percent of all teen deaths in the United States are because of car accidents. There are a number of reasons for this:

- Teens don't have as much experience as older drivers.
- Teens are more likely to take chances when driving, go too fast, and not pay attention to the road.
- Teens may not use their seatbelts regularly.

When you get behind the wheel of a car, you're controlling a ton or two of metal and machinery. That's something to respect.

You may be a careful driver, but pay attention when you're a passenger as well. Many of the teens killed in car accidents were passengers in someone else's car. Experts say that teen drivers are more likely to be in an accident if they have passengers.

What's Happening?

Health issues for females:

- Diet, sleep, and exercise
- Reproductive health
- Sexually transmitted diseases
- Alcohol, drugs, and cigarettes
- Car accidents

7

Birth Control: Having a Baby Can Wait

When a man and a woman have sexual intercourse, they may make a baby. If you don't want to have a baby, you need to protect yourself by using some kind of birth control. **Contraception** is doing something to keep a baby from being made; **contraceptives** are drugs or devices that prevent pregnancy.

Most kinds of birth control are used by women, although there are a few for men. If you use birth control regularly, following the directions your doctor or the package tells you, you probably won't make a baby, but only one kind of birth control is guaranteed to work all the time.

Most birth control needs to be prescribed by a doctor, but there are some things you can buy at a drugstore without a prescription, and you can behave in certain ways to make it less likely that you will make a baby.

Abstinence

Abstinence—not having sexual intercourse at all—is the only birth control that never fails. Some teens choose abstinence because they want to make sure they don't get pregnant, or make anyone else pregnant. Others choose it because it fits with their beliefs.

Many parents would like their kids to decide to be abstinent because they hope they will wait to have sexual intercourse until they are older.

It can be harder than you think to choose abstinence, because movies, magazines, books, television shows, and music seem to encourage having sex. You don't hear many songs about waiting to have sex until you are ready. Some teens think that being abstinent makes you strange.

If you choose to be abstinent, look for people and activities that support your decision. Some religious congregations have groups for teens who choose abstinence.

Abstinence only works if you *stay* abstinent. If you are abstinent for a while, then have intercourse, then are abstinent again, you can get pregnant.

Barrier Contraceptives

Barrier contraceptives keep sperm from getting to an egg. Some of them are real barriers, made of plastic or latex. A few kill sperm, using chemicals.

Condoms

Condoms or **rubbers** are probably the oldest birth control. They fit over the penis, so when a man ejaculates, the tip of the condom collects the semen and no sperm can get into a woman's vagina. Condoms come in packets that make them look almost like large coins. A condom is put on over an erect penis (you center it on the tip, then roll it out down the sides of the penis). When a condom is rolled over an erect penis, it looks like a balloon. You can buy condoms without a prescription in drugstores and grocery stores.

Often, there are machines selling condoms in the men's rooms of stores, restaurants, and gas stations. Condoms are used for birth control and as protection against sexually transmitted diseases.

A **female condom** goes inside a woman's vagina so that when she has sexual intercourse, no sperm can get into her vagina. They are a little more complicated to use than a condom that goes over the penis. You can buy female condoms without a prescription at the drugstore.

Spermicides

Spermicides are chemicals that kill sperm before they can get to an egg. You can use a spermicide with another kind of barrier birth control, just to make sure there won't be a pregnancy. Usually there is an applicator for the spermicide. A woman puts the spermicide into her vagina before having sexual intercourse. **Nonoxynol-9** is a spermicide that can be used as a cream, a **contraceptive foam,** or a jelly.

Diaphragm

A **diaphragm, cervical cap,** or **shield** is a small rubber or plastic device that goes high into the vagina and fits over the cervix so that sperm can't get to an egg. A diaphragm has to be prescribed by a doctor because it needs to fit the right way or it will not protect against pregnancy.

Usually, a spermicide is used with the diaphragm.

Contraceptive Sponge

You can buy **contraceptive sponges** at the drugstore without a prescription. It's a soft device, like a sponge, that is put into the vagina before having sexual intercourse. The sponge has spermicide in it. In the vagina, the sponge expands a bit, keeping sperm from getting to an egg.

Hormone-Based Contraceptives

Many of the most popular contraceptives use hormones to keep an egg from developing into a baby. They are all used by women, although scientists are trying to make contraceptives that men could use to keep from getting someone pregnant.

The main advantage of hormone-based contraceptives is that they are very good at keeping a woman from getting pregnant. They do not protect against sexually transmitted diseases. Some women have uncomfortable side effects from the hormones.

Birth Control Pills

Birth control pills or "**the pill**" are pills that a woman takes to keep from getting pregnant. The hormones in birth control pills can do several different things to prevent pregnancy:

- Keep the ovaries from releasing an egg. Without an egg, there can't be a pregnancy.
- Change the inside of the vagina so that sperm can't get to an egg.
- Keep an egg from settling into the mucus in the cervix.

The **emergency contraceptive pill** or the **morning-after pill** can be used after intercourse, if a woman thinks she might become pregnant. The pill uses hormones to keep an egg from settling into the lining of the uterus. The morning-after pill can be taken within a couple of days of having intercourse. It's available without a prescription, but not to women under eighteen.

The morning-after pill is for emergencies. It shouldn't be used for regular birth control.

Other Hormone-Based Contraceptives

Some hormone-based contraceptives are put in the vagina or even on an arm. They release small amounts of hormones all the time. The advantage of these contraceptives is that a woman doesn't have to think about them all the time. They stay in place for weeks or even months. These include:

- **Contraceptive patch.** A patch that releases hormones through the skin. It's often just called "the patch." Women usually have the patch on a shoulder or somewhere else where it can't be seen easily. The patch keeps the ovaries from releasing eggs.
- **Contraceptive implant.** A contraceptive implant is a tiny device that is put just under the skin at the top of a woman's arm. It releases hormones slowly and keeps the ovaries from releasing eggs.
- **Contraceptive ring.** The contraceptive ring is put into the vagina. It stays in place for about three weeks, then is taken out when a woman has her menstrual period. It keeps the ovaries from releasing an egg and also changes the mucus in the cervix so that an egg won't settle in.
- **Contraceptive injection.** Some women get an injection or shot of hormones about every three months, to keep from getting pregnant. They like the idea that they don't have to put anything in their vaginas and that their protection lasts for three months.

Intrauterine Birth Control

An **intrauterine device** or **IUD** is a small plastic device that is put into the uterus by a doctor. Most IUDs have hormones in them. Some also have a little bit of copper. They can protect against pregnancy for as long as ten years.

IUDs work by killing sperm and by changing the lining of the uterus so that eggs can't settle in and start a baby.

IUDs are used mostly by women who already have had a child. They are recommended for women who are in a relationship with just one man.

Natural Birth Control

Some people don't want to use birth control that involves chemicals or devices. They may have religious reasons for this, or they may just not like the idea of "artificial" birth control. Some **natural birth control** methods can be good at preventing pregnancy—but only if you do them *exactly* the right way.

Coitus Interruptus

Coitus interruptus, also called the **pullout method** of birth control or **withdrawal**, is when the man pulls his penis out of a woman's vagina just before ejaculating. The idea is that the sperm never get into the woman's vagina, so they can't get to an egg. That's not always true. A tiny bit of semen, with sperm in it, sometimes comes out of the penis even before ejaculation.

Rhythm Method

A woman ovulates, or releases an egg, once every twenty-eight days or so. The only time she can get pregnant is when there is an egg ready to meet with a sperm, just after she ovulates. By keeping track of when she ovulates, the woman and her partner can choose to have sex only during times when she is not ovulating.

The **rhythm method**, or **fertility awareness method** of birth control (also called the **temperature method, ovulation method,** or **calendar method**), is a way to keep track of ovulation so that a couple can avoid having sex during a woman's most fertile time of the month. During ovulation a woman's vaginal discharge may be thicker and her temperature may be higher. Ovulation usually happens about fourteen days before a woman's period starts.

By watching **basal body temperature** and vaginal mucus, and keeping close track of when a woman's periods start, a woman and her partner can figure out when she is likely to be ovulating. If they don't have sex for about a week during that time, they may avoid a pregnancy.

The rhythm method is not as good as other methods for preventing pregnancy, partly because it must be followed exactly and partly because sometimes a woman's body changes and it's harder to tell when she's ovulating. It's usually not a good method of birth control for sexually active young people.

Lactational Amenorrhea Method

When a woman is nursing a baby, she is less likely to ovulate for about six months after the baby is born. The **lactational amenorrhea method** relies on nursing as birth control. This is not good birth control, since some women begin to ovulate even while they are still nursing.

Permanent Birth Control

After they have had all the children they want, or after they have decided they don't ever want to have children, some people choose to have surgery so that they can never get pregnant or make someone pregnant. This is called **sterilization**.

A **vasectomy** seals the ends of the **vas deferens** in a man so that no sperm go into the penis. The testicles still make sperm, but they just break down after a little while and the body absorbs them.

A vasectomy can sometimes be reversed so that sperm will be released again, but no man should have a vasectomy unless he is sure he doesn't want to have children.

If a woman wants sterilization, she can have a **tubal ligation**. In this surgery, the doctor ties, cuts, or seals the woman's Fallopian tubes so that no eggs can move into the uterus. Tubal ligations can be reversed, but the success rate can vary.

What's Happening?

Types of birth control:

- Abstinence
- Barrier methods
- Hormone-based methods
- Intrauterine devices
- Natural methods
- Permanent methods

8

Pregnancy and Birth: It's a Baby!

As a young person, it's smart for you to put off having a baby for at least a few years, until you are ready to be responsible for taking care of a baby. But it's good to understand how a baby is created and how it grows before it is born. You may hear people talk about "the miracle of birth." Plenty of humans have babies—they've always had babies; otherwise we wouldn't be here. But the story of creating and growing a baby is kind of amazing, no matter how many times it's been done.

Starting with the Sperm and the Egg

Conception is when a male sperm and a female egg begin to make a baby. To **conceive** is to become pregnant. Human **reproduction** means "reproducing" human life—or making more of it.

Usually, sperm come out of a man's penis in a woman's vagina during sexual intercourse. The sperm go through the cervix and the uterus, into the Fallopian tubes. If there is an egg in one of the Fallopian tubes, a sperm may touch it and then go right into it. When one sperm enters the egg, the egg's wall changes so that no other sperm can come in. **Fertilization** is when the sperm enters the egg.

If a woman has trouble getting pregnant, or if she doesn't have a male partner, she may use **artificial insemination** to help her conceive. For artificial insemination, a doctor uses semen that has been provided by a woman's partner or donated by someone else. The semen is put high into the woman's vagina, where it has a good chance of making it to an egg.

Not many years ago, doctors discovered ways to bring an egg and sperm together outside the body. A woman is given hormones that will help her release several eggs. These eggs are removed from her Fallopian tubes and put in liquid in a small container. Sperm are put in the container with the eggs. When the sperm and eggs have come together and begun to grow, one or more are put back into the woman's uterus. This process is called **in vitro fertilization**, which means fertilization in an artificial environment. Children who were born after their parents used this way to conceive originally were called "**test tube babies.**"

A woman who is able to have children, and a man whose sperm can make children, are **fertile**. Their **fertility** means that if they don't want to have children, they need to be careful about birth control when having sexual intercourse. Some people can't get pregnant when they want to. Either the woman or the man trying to conceive could have a problem. This **infertility** can be temporary, or it can be something that will not change. Luckily, there is more than one way to have a baby in your life.

Your Parents Made You

Many of the things that make you the person you are come from your mother or your father. Blue eyes or brown? Curly hair or straight? Tall or short? Loud voice or soft? You have dozens and dozens of **inherited traits,** some that you can see and some that you can't. This is your **heredity** from your **father** and **mother**—and from their fathers and mothers before them. That's why people may say you look just like your grandfather, or your great-aunt Sue.

The study of how humans inherit different traits is called **genetics.**

A **cell** is the smallest part of your body. You have trillions of cells. Cells take in material from food and turn it into energy—which is what we call life. Different cells have different roles—cells in your skin do different things than the cells in your heart, for example. **DNA,** or **deoxyribonucleic acid,** is the material that carries your heredity. Almost every cell in your body has the same DNA, even though what they do is very different.

Genes are made up of DNA. Strings of genes are called **chromosomes.** Normally, genes come in pairs. Every cell in your body has a pair of genes for each trait. A sperm or an egg only has one gene for each trait. When the sperm and the egg come together, the fertilized egg becomes a **zygote,** with a pair of genes for each trait. From your mother, you have **maternal** genes and traits. From your father, you have **paternal** genes and traits.

Some genes are for **recessive traits,** which mean that a trait will only show up if the other gene in the pair is the same. For example: Blue eyes are a recessive trait. If you have blue eyes, both of the eye-color genes you have are for blue. If you have one blue eye-color gene and one brown eye-color gene, your eyes will be brown. (Eye color is a **physical trait,** a characteristic that affects how you look.)

Some illnesses or problems are recessive traits. They don't show up until a woman carrying the gene for the trait and a man carrying the gene for the trait—who may not have the problem themselves—create a baby with both genes for the recessive trait.

A disease or problem that has been inherited is not the same as a **congenital** problem.

Doctors recommend **genetic counseling** for some people before they get pregnant, to check for the possibility of an inherited trait that can be a problem.

One Cell Becomes a Baby

Less than an hour after an egg is fertilized by a sperm, it splits in half and becomes two cells, and then those cells split and become four and so on. The early stages of a baby's development are:

- **Zygote.** The zygote is the fertilized egg in the Fallopian tube.
- **Morula.** About three or four days after being fertilized, the egg has become about sixteen cells and is now a morula. It has moved through the Fallopian tube to the uterus.
- **Blastocyst.** About five days after fertilization, the group of cells becomes a blastocyst, which settles into the lining of the uterus. This is called **implantation**. The cells in the blastocyst start to become different things as they divide and make more cells. This process of **cell division** is called **differentiation**. Part of the differentiated cells will continue to grow into a baby and part will grow into the **placenta**, which supplies blood from the mother to the baby.
- **Embryo.** About two weeks after fertilization, the group of cells begins to have a shape. From two weeks until about two months, this stage of development is called an embryo.

- **Fetus.** From about two months after fertilization until birth, the developing baby is called a fetus.
- **Baby.** A baby is a child that has just been born. We often call a fetus a baby, just because people tend to get attached

Once inside the uterus, the developing baby is surrounded by the **amniotic sac,** a thin layer of tissue (**amnion**) filled with **amniotic fluid,** so the fetus is sort of floating within it. The amniotic sac helps protect the developing baby from being hurt. The outer layer of the amniotic sac is called the **chorion.**

The placenta is an organ that is inside a woman only while she's pregnant. It forms to supply the fetus with blood and to take away its waste. The fetus is connected to the placenta through the **umbilical cord,** which goes into the fetus through what will become its **belly button** or **navel.**

As the weeks go by, the fetus becomes more and more of a baby. Four weeks after fertilization, the embryo only has the beginning of a head and spots where its eyes will be. By twelve weeks, it has a heart and its bones are beginning to form. By five months, it has muscles and you may feel it kicking and moving. By twenty-eight weeks, it weighs about four pounds.

More Than One?

Normally, one sperm fertilizes one egg and one baby is created. But sometimes a woman can be pregnant with more than one baby. Two babies, or **twins,** can be created in two ways:

- The woman releases two eggs, which are fertilized by two sperm, so two zygotes are created. These grow into two fetuses that are related, but have differences in their genes. These are **fraternal twins.**

- One egg is fertilized by one sperm and then splits into two separate cells. These two cells have exactly the same genes, so the two babies that are created will be **identical twins**.

Very rarely, a zygote doesn't split all the way as identical twins are being formed. The two babies will be born connected to each other. That connection can be at almost any place on the body. These **conjoined twins** or **Siamese twins** can sometimes, but not always, be separated through surgery.

It is possible to have more than two babies. When a woman has three or more babies, they may be fraternal, identical, or a combination of fraternal and identical. Women who take drugs to help them get pregnant, or who use in vitro fertilization, are more likely to have more than one baby at a time.

Tests

A number of tests can be done while a woman is pregnant, to make sure the baby is doing all right:

- An **ultrasound** is a safe way to look at the fetus. Vibrations, kind of like sound waves, bounce off the growing fetus and show a "picture" of it. It shows how large the fetus is, which helps determine when it will be born. Sometimes—but not always—an ultrasound can show whether the fetus is male or female.
- To check for some kinds of birth defects, a doctor may do **amniocentesis**. A needle is put in through the abdomen to take out a little bit of the amniotic fluid so that it can be tested.
- **Chorionic villi sampling** or **CVS** also takes a sample from the amniotic sac. A thin tube is put into the woman's vagina, then up into the uterus. A tiny

sample of the outer layer of the uterus, the chorion, is removed and tested. This can be done earlier than amniocentesis, when there might be a serious problem.

- A **fetoscopy** looks directly at the fetus. A small instrument is put into the amniotic cavity, where the amniotic sac sits, through a tiny hole in the woman's abdomen.

Pregnancy

It takes about forty weeks, or a little over nine months, to go from the meeting of sperm and egg to the birth of a baby. That period of time is called **pregnancy**. A woman with a baby growing inside her is **pregnant**.

We often talk about pregnancy as having three parts, each called a **trimester**. Different things happen both to the mother and to the baby inside during each trimester.

Once an egg has been fertilized by a sperm, it settles into the lining of the uterus and begins to grow. This is called implantation. (Once in a while, the baby starts to grow in the Fallopian tube, instead of the uterus. This is an **ectopic pregnancy** or a **tubal pregnancy**. This can be very dangerous for the mother.)

A woman may be pregnant for a month or longer before she realizes it. The first signs of pregnancy may be her breasts getting larger and sore, missing a period, and feeling sick to her stomach (**morning sickness**—although it doesn't just happen in the morning).

When the woman goes to a doctor who will help her through her pregnancy—an **obstetrician**—the doctor will test her for **human chorionic gonadotropin**, or **HCG**, a hormone that pregnant women have. If she is pregnant, the doctor will find her **due date**, the day the baby will be born, by counting forty weeks from the start of her last menstrual period. The baby is in **gestation**, or growing, during those forty weeks.

What happens before a baby is born is called **prenatal**. Around the time the baby is born, and just after, is **perinatal**.

Once a woman is pregnant, she should have regular **prenatal care** from an obstetrician or a **midwife** (a nurse who has been trained especially to help women through pregnancy and birth). At least once, and maybe several times, she will have an ultrasound, which safely shows the baby growing inside.

Stages of Pregnancy

FIRST TRIMESTER

A woman may not notice many changes during the first month to six weeks of a pregnancy. After that, she may notice changes that include:

- Feeling tired
- Occasional faintness
- Needing to urinate a lot
- Morning sickness
- Headaches
- Heavier vaginal discharge

The pregnant woman's hormones are changing, and the baby is growing quickly during the first trimester.

SECOND TRIMESTER

For many women, this is the nicest time during pregnancy. Morning sickness usually goes away. Although the woman is gaining weight, she can still move around easily. She may feel a lot of energy. At about the middle of this trimester, she can start to feel the baby move inside her, called **quickening**.

Because the baby is getting much bigger, the last trimester can be hard on some women. A pregnant woman may notice:

- Backaches
- Needing to urinate often because the baby is now pressing against her bladder
- **Hemorrhoids,** which happen when veins in the rectum get too large
- Swelling in the ankles, feet, and legs
- Leg cramps
- Leaking breasts

Problems in Pregnancy
Most women have healthy pregnancies and babies, but there are problems that can come up:

- **Miscarriage.** Sometimes the baby dies and the pregnancy ends. Often, there seems to be no reason for the end of the pregnancy, although some researchers think that a miscarriage happens when there is something wrong with the baby. Most miscarriages happen during the first three months of pregnancy. Some women may have a miscarriage before they know they are pregnant.
- **Pregnancy-induced hypertension.** A woman's blood pressure may get higher during pregnancy, called pregnancy-induced hypertension. A pregnant woman's blood pressure is checked at every prenatal visit, so her doctor can see any early signs of hypertension. Hypertension can become **toxemia** or **preeclampsia,** a very dangerous condition toward the end of pregnancy. If

not treated, the baby and the mother can die. Once the baby is born, the hypertension disappears.

- **Gestational diabetes.** Some women develop gestational diabetes during pregnancy. Their blood-sugar levels become very high, but go back to normal after the baby is born.
- **Exposure to teratogens.** A teratogen is anything that might make a pregnancy go wrong or lead to a miscarriage. Cigarettes, alcohol, some diseases or chemicals may all be teratogens.

In Sympathy

Although men can't get pregnant, sometimes a woman's male partner acts as if he is carrying a baby, too. He gains weight, he feels sick to his stomach—he may even say he can feel a baby moving inside him. This condition, called **sympathetic pregnancy** or **couvade syndrome**, happens to a number of men. They really want to share the experience of pregnancy, so their minds and bodies make them think they are pregnant.

Giving Birth

After more than nine months of being pregnant, most women are ready to have their baby and begin being a parent. They're tired of carrying that baby around inside. Giving **birth**, or **parturition**, is not easy, but women have been doing it for as long as there have been human beings. It's a natural thing.

Options

In **natural childbirth**, a woman will not use any drugs as she's having the baby. There are several different kinds of natural childbirth, each with different breathing exercises and training to help a woman control any pain she feels. The **Bradley method,** the **Lamaze method,** and the **Leboyer method** are all well-known forms of natural childbirth. (In the Leboyer method, the baby is born in a quiet room with dim light and is put on its mother's abdomen right after birth.)

Many women choose to have less pain during childbirth by using drugs. For an **epidural block,** medication is put into the woman's spine. It blocks pain in the lower part of the woman's body. A **saddle block** also blocks pain through the spine. A **paracervical block** is medication put into the area near the cervix.

Sometimes a baby can't be born through the vagina. In that case, a **Cesarean section,** or **C-section,** will be done. A C-section is surgery through the abdomen. A doctor will open the uterus and take the baby out. When a baby seems to be in trouble, the doctor may do an emergency C-section to get it out quickly.

Labor Begins

Uterine contractions may be the first sign that a woman is ready to give birth. These **contractions** feel as if the uterus is squeezing itself tight. (Sometimes a woman will have **Braxton Hicks contractions** or **false labor** before she is ready to have the baby.) When a woman begins having contractions, she is in **labor,** meaning that she is starting to give birth to her baby.

Labor can go on for hours. Some women give birth only a couple of hours after starting labor. Many are in labor for six, eight, twelve, or even twenty hours. The doctor or midwife makes sure that both the mother and the baby are okay during labor.

While a woman is in labor, the opening to the uterus, the cervix, is stretching and getting thinner so that a baby can come through it. Its opening is called **dilation.** The thinning out is called **effacement.** When the cervix is completely dilated, the baby can move into the vagina—which is sometimes called the **birth canal** when a baby is coming out. (It's hard to believe that the narrow vagina can open wide enough to have a baby come through, but it stretches. Think of pulling on a turtleneck sweater.)

The baby should come through the vagina head first, but sometimes it is not turned in that direction. If the baby's feet or rear end come down the vagina first, it's a **breech birth.** This is dangerous for both the baby and the mother. The doctor or mid-wife will try to turn the baby into the right position. If that can't be done, the baby will be delivered by a C-section.

As the baby comes through the vagina, a doctor may make a cut in the opening to the vagina so that the baby can come through more easily. This cut is called an **episiotomy.**

After the baby is born, the umbilical cord connecting it to the placenta is cut and clamped. A little while later, the placenta will come out. This is often called the **afterbirth.**

The doctor or midwife or nurse will take the **newborn** baby and give it a quick exam to make sure it's okay. The baby's weight and length are recorded. The **infant** will be covered with a creamy white coating at first; usually nurses rub the baby with a blanket to clean it up. There will be a soft spot in the baby's head, the **fontanel,** that will close up a few weeks after birth.

Problems

Some things can go wrong during pregnancy or during the baby's birth. These possible problems include:

- **Stillbirth.** Sometimes a fetus dies before or while it is being born. When that baby comes out of the woman's body, it's called a stillbirth.
- **Premature baby.** A baby that is born too soon is a premature baby, or **preemie.** The closer to forty weeks, the healthier the baby is likely to be.

- **Prolapsed cord.** Sometimes during birth, the umbilical cord becomes wrapped around the baby's neck. This can cut off the baby's breath. If the doctor finds a prolapsed cord, the baby may be born by C-section.
- **Birth disorder or birth defect.** Some babies have a big or small problem when they are born. This is a birth disorder or a birth defect, because it is there at birth.
- **Rh incompatibility.** Everyone has a factor in their blood that is either Rh-positive or Rh-negative. If a mother who is Rh-negative has a fetus that is Rh-positive, her body may make antibodies that can hurt other babies she may have. It's easy to prevent Rh incompatibility with a shot of gamma globulin.
- **Fetal alcohol syndrome.** If a woman drinks alcohol while she is pregnant, it may permanently damage her fetus. Babies born with fetal alcohol syndrome may have developmental disabilities or physical problems.

Right after Birth

Right after a baby is born, during the **postpartum** period, men and women start learning how to be parents. Some of it comes naturally; some has to be learned. **Parenting** is the most important thing a man or woman can do.

Some women find themselves very sad after their baby is born. They're embarrassed to tell anyone about it, because they think they ought to be happy. These **baby blues** can be normal—after all, life has just changed a lot, the mother probably isn't getting the kind of sleep she needs, she can't go anywhere without her baby, she wants to lose weight, and she's still unsure of how to take care of the baby. Baby blues can turn into serious **postpartum depression** for a few women. A woman who feels like she's "losing it," or who is afraid she might hurt her baby or herself, should get help right away.

Feeding the Baby

A woman's body is made to feed her baby. Glands in her breasts make **milk** that is all her baby has to have to grow and be healthy for many months.

When a baby is first born, the mother's breasts make **colostrum**. This is not milk, but it is full of antibodies that help protect the baby until the mother's milk "comes in." After a few days, the mother's breasts make milk. Making milk is called **lactogenesis**.

A baby will begin to suck at its mother's nipples, or **nurse**, when it is put up to its mother's breast. For most babies, **breastfeeding** is the healthiest way to give them food in the early months of their lives.

Some women can't breastfeed, or think that it is too hard or unpleasant. In the United States, there are many kinds of **formula** that can be used instead of breastfeeding. Many, many happy, healthy babies were raised on formula.

Important Choices

What does a woman do when she finds out she's pregnant—and doesn't want to be? This can be the most important decision she ever has to make, and for most women it is very hard.

Many women choose to have the baby and to raise it, even though they didn't plan to be pregnant.

Some women choose to have the baby and to put it up for **adoption** so that it can be raised by other people who are ready to have a child.

Some women choose to have an **abortion**. An abortion is the removal of an embryo, so the pregnancy is stopped and no baby is born. Most abortions are done during the first three months of pregnancy. They are done at a clinic or hospital.

Abortion is a very difficult issue. Some people believe that abortion of an embryo is killing a child. Others believe that it's not bad to remove an embryo that is not **viable**, which means it is not able to live outside its mother's body.

Abortion is an issue that people disagree about very strongly. Those who are **pro-life** believe that abortion is taking a human life. They believe it should be illegal. Those who are **pro-choice** believe that a woman should have the right to choose abortion as an option for a pregnancy she doesn't want.

Abortion is legal in the United States, but different states have different rules about it. In some states, girls under a certain age need their parents' or guardians' permission to have an abortion. In others, abortions for fetuses past three months old are restricted.

What most people agree on is that it would be better if women did not get pregnant when they don't want to. Abstinence or birth control can help a woman avoid having to make a painful decision.

What's Happening?

How a baby is born:

- Genetic traits
- A cell divides
- Baby's development
- Mother's pregnancy
- Birth

Dictionary

abdomen (AB-doe-men). The part of the body that houses, among other organs, the stomach, the intestines, and, in a female, the uterus.

abortion (a-BORE-shun). The removal of an unborn embryo from a mother's uterus. This procedure is usually done in a doctor's office or a hospital.

abstinence (AB-stih-nens). The act of abstaining, or not doing, something, including sex. Many people practice abstinence from sexual intercourse as a way to prevent pregnancy.

abusive relationship (ah-BYOO-siv ree-LAY-shun-ship). When one or both people in a relationship do things that harm the other. The abuse can include hurting someone physically, such as hitting the person, or hurting her or him by constantly criticizing or saying negative things.

acne (ACK-nee). Pimples; eruptions on the skin common during adolescence and sometimes caused by infections in the pores.

acquaintance rape (uh-QUAYNT-ens rape). Rape, or forced sex, by a person who knows or has met the victim. Also called date rape.

acquired immunodeficiency syndrome (uh-QUI-urd im-YOU-no-dee-FISH-en-see sin-drome) or **AIDS.** A deadly viral disease that causes the immune system to fail. It can be transmitted through sex, needles, or from an infected mother to her unborn baby.

Adam's apple. The projection or bump on a boy's throat that gets bigger as he becomes a man. Girls have them, too, but they are seldom large. It's the part of the throat that contains the vocal cords.

addiction (ah-DICK-shun). A need or dependence on something. Someone who has an addiction to drugs or alcohol needs to keep using drugs or alcohol or he or she will become ill.

adolescence (add-oh-LESS-ens). The time of life when a girl changes into a young woman and a boy changes into a young man. These changes usually begin to take place between ages eight and thirteen and can continue until a person is a legal adult.

adoption. The legal process an adult or adults undergo to receive a child that someone else gave birth to, and raise the child as his, her, or their own. When a woman becomes pregnant and does not want to keep the baby, she can put the baby up for adoption.

adultery (uh-DULL-tuh-ree). Sexual intercourse between a married person and someone other than his or her spouse.

affection (uh-FECK-shun). Caring for something or someone.

afterbirth. Shortly after a baby is born, the placenta, a temporary organ, is expelled from the mother. This is called the afterbirth.

AIDS. *See* acquired immunodeficiency syndrome.

alcohol poisoning. Drinking so much alcohol in a short period of time that it harms a person physically. Alcohol poisoning can affect breathing and the heart and may cause coma and death if the person doesn't get medical attention right away.

alcoholism (AL-coh-hall-ism). An ongoing need to drink alcohol, even though it may be harming the drinker's life and health.

amenorrhea (a-MEN-uh-REE-uh). Absence of menstruation. The primary form is when a female, age sixteen or older, has not had her first menstrual period. The secondary form is when a female's menstruation cycle ceases. In both cases, the female should see a physician about possible problems with her reproductive system.

amniocentesis (AM-nee-oh-sen-TEE-sis). A medical procedure in which a doctor inserts a hollow needle through the abdomen and into the uterus of a pregnant female and withdraws amniotic fluid. This can be done to determine the sex of the unborn child, check chemicals that determine mature fetal lung development, or check for abnormal chromosomes.

amnion (AM-nee-ahn). The inner layer of tissue of the amniotic sac.

amniotic fluid (am-nee-AH-tik fluid). The fluid surrounding an unborn child inside the mother's uterus.

amniotic sac (am-nee-AH-tik sac). A thin membrane that forms a closed sac around the fetus inside the mother's uterus. It contains the amniotic fluid.

anal intercourse (A-nul IN-ter-kors) or **anal sex** (A-nul seks). The insertion of a man's penis into the anus of another person for sexual stimulation.

anorexia nervosa (ann-a-REX-ee-uh ner-VOS-uh). An eating disorder in which a person becomes obsessed with losing weight and engages in dangerous behavior, such as starvation; use of pills, laxatives, or diuretics; and obsessive calorie counting and exercise. If not addressed, it can lead to serious illness and even death.

antibodies (AN-tih-body). Proteins produced in the blood in response to toxins or foreign organisms. In many cases, antibodies can neutralize toxins and help eliminate infections. When a person has AIDS, though, antibodies cannot combat disease.

anus (A-nus). The opening in the body through which bowel movements pass.

areolae (ah-REE-oh-lay). On a woman's breasts, the areas of darkened skin surrounding the nipples. The singular form is areola.

arousal (uh-ROU-zal). Feelings of strong physical attraction toward another person; sexual excitement.

arranged marriage. In some cultures, parents or others choose partners for their children, instead of the young people finding their own husband or wife. Sometimes, a couple may not meet each other until their wedding day.

artificial insemination (ar-tih-FISH-ul in-sem-ih-NAY-shun). A medical procedure in which semen is placed into the vagina using a syringe. This is done to help a woman get pregnant when attempts to conceive through intercourse have failed.

B

baby. A newborn child.

baby blues. *See* postpartum depression.

Bartholin's glands (BAR-tuh-linz glands). Two small glands in the vagina that secrete a fluid that lubricates the vagina when a female is sexually aroused.

basal body temperature. The temperature of the body when waking from sleep. A woman can keep track of this daily to help her determine when she is ovulating.

belly button. The scar left on a baby's abdomen when the umbilical cord is cut at birth. Also called the navel.

binge drinking (binj drinking). Drinking a large number of alcoholic beverages in a short amount of time, in order to get drunk. Some experts consider five drinks at one time for a man or four drinks for a woman to be binge drinking.

binge eating (binj eating). An eating disorder similar to compulsive overeating, in which a person frequently and compulsively eats an unusually large amount of food in a short period of time. Binge episodes usually occur two or more times a week. This behavior can result in serious health problems, including obesity and high blood pressure. *See also* compulsive overeating.

birth. The process that brings a baby into the world. After nine months in the uterus, the baby comes out of the mother's body through the birth canal.

birth canal. Refers to the vagina because it is the baby's passageway from the mother's uterus to the outside world.

birth control. Any method used to prevent pregnancy. One example is birth control pills. *See* contraception.

birth control pills. Pills taken by a woman to prevent pregnancy. They contain hormones that either prevent ovulation, thicken cervical mucus to prevent sperm from reaching an egg, or both.

birth disorder or **birth defect.** An abnormality of structure, function, or body metabolism that is present at birth. It may be minor or serious, and may be caused by genetic, environmental, or unknown factors.

bisexual (by-SEKS-you-uhl). A person who is sexually attracted to both sexes, male and female.

bladder. The sac in the body where urine is stored.

blastocyst (BLAST-oh-sist). The third stage in the development of a baby inside the mother's body. This is the term for the development stage that starts about five days after the sperm fertilizes the ovum (egg), and continues until about the fourteenth day. During this stage, the fertilized ovum travels through the Fallopian tube to the uterus and attaches (implants) itself to the uterine wall, called the endometrium.

body fluids. Any fluids that exist normally in the body, such as blood, semen, and vaginal secretions.

body image. The way a person feels about and sees his or her own body. During puberty and adolescence, body image can become a major issue because young people are often uncomfortable with all the changes their bodies are going through. If a poor body image isn't dealt with in a healthy way, it can lead to such problems as low self-esteem, eating disorders, and depression.

body odor. Odor created by perspiration combined with natural bacteria on the skin. It may begin to be noticeable during puberty, when sweat glands become more active. Bathing daily with soap and water—and using deodorant if needed—usually prevents the odor.

bosom (BUHZ-em). A woman's breasts; a man's chest.

Bradley method. A method of natural childbirth developed by Dr. Robert Bradley. The technique emphasizes abdominal breathing techniques designed to help a mother relax during childbirth.

Braxton Hicks contractions. *See* false labor.

breast self-examination (BSE). A technique developed to help a woman check for lumps or changes in the breasts. The purpose of this is to detect breast cancer in its earliest stages, when it is more likely to be successfully treated.

breastfeeding. The feeding of a baby from a mother's breasts rather than from a bottle. Also called nursing.

breasts. Two glands on a female's chest that begin to develop and grow during puberty, sometime between ages eight and thirteen. Their primary purpose is to provide nourishment to a woman's baby; a mother's milk develops in them soon after her child is born. They also play a role in sex, as a female may become aroused when her breasts are touched, and a male may become aroused when he sees or touches a female's breasts. Also called mammary glands.

breech birth. When a baby comes through the birth canal buttocks or feet first, rather than head first as in a normal birth. This can be dangerous for both the mother and the baby. Therefore, the doctor or midwife will try to reposition the baby so that the head will come out first. If that isn't possible, a doctor will deliver the baby by Cesarean section.

bulbourethral glands (bul-boe-you-REE-thrul glands). *See* Cowper's glands.

bulimia nervosa (buh-LEE-mee-uh ner-VOS-uh). An eating disorder in which a person engages in binge eating and then purging to prevent gaining weight. The purging can be done in a variety of ways, including self-induced vomiting and abuse of diuretics or laxatives. It can lead to serious health problems.

buttocks (BUHT-ocks). The rump; the part of the body a person sits on.

C

calendar method. A fertility awareness or "rhythm" method of birth control in which a woman keeps track of the dates of her menstrual cycles. This helps her determine when she is ovulating.

calories (CAL-oh-rees). A unit of energy. Food produces energy, which is released when eaten. Most people need 1,500 to 2,400 calories each day, depending on their age, gender, and activity. When someone eats more calories than his or her body uses, the extra calories are stored and then turn to fat.

carbohydrates (kar-boh-HY-draytz). Sugars and starches in food that the body breaks down into simple sugars, which go into the bloodstream. Complex carbohydrates, like brown rice or oatmeal, give energy over a long time. Simple sugars break down in the body quickly, so the person may feel hungry again quickly.

celibate (SELL-ih-but). Someone who chooses not to have sexual intercourse.

cell. A tiny, microscopic piece of matter capable of interacting with other cells to perform the functions of life.

cell division. The process by which cells multiply. Also the process by which a new baby is formed in the body of the mother.

cervical cap (SER-vih-kuhl cap). A barrier method of contraception in which a small rubber or plastic cap fits snugly over the cervix to block sperm from entering.

cervical mucus (SER-vih-kal MYOO-kus). A sticky substance surrounding the opening of the cervix or neck of the womb.

cervical os (SER-vih-kal ohs). The opening of the cervix.

cervix (SER-vix). The narrow opening or neck of the uterus. It expands to allow a baby to be born.

Cesarean section (se-ZAIR-ee-an section). A surgical operation to deliver a baby from the uterus through the mother's abdomen. This is necessary when a baby is not able to be born naturally through the mother's vagina.

chancre (SHANK-er). A small sore or ulcer; can be a symptom of syphilis. *See* syphilis.

change of life. *See* menopause.

chaste (CHASED). Someone who is modest, pure, innocent, or who does not have sexual relations before marriage.

chlamydia (kla-MIH-dee-ah). A bacterial infection that causes nongonococcal urethritis, a common sexually transmitted disease. In women, it is a leading cause of Fallopian tube damage and infertility.

chorion (KOR-ee-ahn). The outer layer of tissue of the amniotic sac.

chorionic villi sampling (KOR-ee-ahn-ick VILL-ee samp-ling) or **CVS.** A medical procedure in which a doctor inserts a thin tube into a pregnant female's vagina, through her cervix, and into her uterus to take a sample of the outer layer of the amniotic sac (called the chorion). The sample can help determine whether the developing fetus has any birth defects. This test can be done as early as the second month of pregnancy.

chromosome (CROME-a-zome). Part of a cell nucleus containing the genes that make up an individual.

circumcision (sir-kum-SIH-shun). The removal of the foreskin from a baby's penis. A doctor performs this operation a few days after a boy is born. Not all parents have this operation performed. Circumcision is a religious custom in the Jewish and Muslim faiths. It is also performed for health reasons, but many doctors now say it is not necessary.

climax (CLY-max). *See* orgasm.

clitoral hood (KLIT-eh-rull hood). A fold of skin covering the clitoris. *See also* prepuce (2).

clitoris (KLIT-eh-res). A small but sensitive part of a woman's sexual organs, located in the vulva above the vaginal opening. Its sexual function is similar to that of the male penis.

coitus (KO-ee-tus). Another name for sexual intercourse.

coitus interruptus (KO-ee-tus in-ter-UP-tus). The male withdraws his penis from the vagina just before ejaculation in an effort to prevent pregnancy. This is not considered to be an effective pregnancy prevention method. Also called withdrawal or pullout method.

colostrum (koh-LOSS-trum). A substance produced by a mother's breasts shortly after a baby is born. It is healthy for the newborn baby to drink the colostrum before the mother's milk "comes in," which usually happens a few days after birth.

compulsive exercising. A disorder in which a person engages in excessive exercise to the point that it interferes with other obligations or pastimes and becomes unhealthy. Excessive exercise often begins as a way for a young person to feel more in control of his or her body and weight. This behavior sometimes accompanies an eating disorder and can lead to serious health problems, including dehydration, stress fractures, reproductive problems, and heart problems.

compulsive overeating. An eating disorder in which a person consistently eats large amounts of food and uses food to cope with sadness, stress, and other emotions. Compulsive overeaters are believed to be addicted to food. The behavior can lead to health problems such as obesity, heart attack, high blood pressure, and high cholesterol.

conceive (con-SEEV). To become pregnant.

conception (con-SEP-shun). The coming together of an egg cell from the mother and a sperm cell from the father. This is the beginning of the development of a new baby.

condom (CON-dum). A soft rubber device that fits over a man's penis. It is worn during intercourse to prevent pregnancy and sexually transmitted diseases. Sometimes called a "rubber."

congenital (con-JEN-ih-tuhl). A condition existing at birth or acquired during development in the uterus; not an inherited trait or condition.

conjoined twins. Twins that are physically connected to one another at birth. This happens when the zygote of identical twins fails to completely separate. Sometimes called Siamese twins.

contraception (con-tra-SEP-shun). Preventing a baby from being conceived.

contraceptive (con-tra-SEP-tiv). Any of a number of methods used to prevent pregnancy, such as the IUD (intrauterine device), condom, diaphragm, "the pill," vasectomy, and tubal ligation.

contraceptive foam (con-tra-SEP-tiv foam). A type of contraceptive that a woman places in her vagina using an applicator. It kills sperm and prevents sperm from reaching the woman's egg.

contraceptive implant. (con-tra-SEP-tive IM-plant). A contraceptive that is surgically inserted into a woman's upper arm. It releases a synthetic form of progesterone into the woman's system to prevent ovulation, thereby preventing pregnancy.

contraceptive injection (con-tra-SEP-tive in-JECK-shun). A hormone injection that a woman gets to prevent pregnancy. The injection, which is effective for three months, contains synthetic progesterone. It prevents pregnancy by preventing ovulation.

contraceptive patch (con-tra-SEP-tive patch). An adhesive patch that releases synthetic estrogen and progestin hormones into the system when placed on the skin. It prevents pregnancy primarily by preventing ovulation.

contraceptive ring (con-tra-SEP-tive ring). A flexible, plastic ring that is placed in the vagina to prevent pregnancy.

This contraceptive works by releasing hormones that prevent ovulation.

contraceptive sponge (con-tra-SEP-tive sponj). A soft, plastic birth-control device containing sperm-killing chemicals. A woman places the sponge in her vagina before intercourse to prevent pregnancy.

contractions (con-TRACK-shuns). The workings of the muscles of the mother's uterus that get stronger and stronger during labor, just before a baby is born. Contractions push a baby into the world.

copulation (cop-you-LAY-shun). Another name for sexual intercourse.

corona (kuh-ROW-nuh). The flared ridge at the back of the glans of the penis.

couvade syndrome (koo-VAHD syndrome). A phenomenon in which the father of a pregnant woman's baby feels some of the same symptoms the woman feels. He may experience nausea, vomiting, bloating, and food cravings. This is also referred to as sympathetic pregnancy.

Cowper's glands (KOW-pers glands). Two small, round glands located underneath a male's prostate gland. When a male is sexually aroused, the glands produce a fluid that lubricates the penis and protects the sperm as it travels through the acidic environment of the urethra. The formal term for these glands is bulbourethral glands.

crabs or **crab lice.** Insects that get into the pubic hair and cause severe itching and, in some cases, slight bleeding. Crabs can be passed from one person to another through genital contact, or by using towels, bedding, or other materials that have been used by an infected person. Also called pubic lice.

C-section. *See* Cesarean section.

D

date rape. *See* acquaintance rape.

date rape drug. A chemical that makes a person unable to know what is happening or remember what has happened. Because the drug is difficult to see or taste, it can easily be put into someone's drink without the person's knowledge. This prevents the victim from resisting or remembering the rape.

dating. A time when two people who have romantic feelings for one another do things together.

deoxyribonucleic acid (dee-OX-ee-RYE-bo-new-CLEE-ik acid) or **DNA.** A chemical in the body that is a basic component of genes. DNA determines what characteristics a baby will inherit from its parents and is sometimes called the "blueprint of life."

diabetes (DIE-uh-BEE-teez). A disease in which the body doesn't make enough insulin, a hormone needed to convert sugar and starches from food into energy.

diaphragm (DYE-a-fram). A rubber or plastic device a woman can place over the cervix to prevent pregnancy.

differentiation (diff-ur-en-she-A-shun). The complicated process used by cells to develop the different body parts of a baby in the uterus.

dilation (die-LAY-shun). The opening of the cervix in order to allow a baby to be born.

discharge (DISS-charj). A liquid that comes out of the body. Often refers to vaginal discharge.

DNA. *See* deoxyribonucleic acid.

dominant trait (DOM-in-ant trait). An inherited trait that overrides another trait such as brown eyes being inherited instead of blue eyes.

douche (DOOSH). A current of water or a commercial solution used to cleanse a body cavity—usually the vagina. Most experts say that it is not necessary to use anything other than soap and water to cleanse the vagina.

drug overdose. Taking so much of a drug—legal or illegal—that it is harmful. An overdose can cause death.

due date. The day a pregnant woman is expected to give birth. The due date is determined by counting forty weeks from the first day of the woman's last period. Only 5 percent of women have a baby on that date.

E

eating disorders. Disorders in which a person becomes ill because of improper eating habits. The most common are anorexia nervosa (self-starvation) and bulimia nervosa (binge eating and purging). These disorders are more common in girls than boys.

ectopic pregnancy (eck-TOP-ik pregnancy). The abnormal implantation of a fertile ovum outside the mother's uterus, such as in a Fallopian tube. *See also* tubal pregnancy.

effacement (Eff-FACE-ment). The thinning of the cervix when a woman is getting ready to deliver a baby.

egg cell. The female reproductive cell. When an egg cell meets with a sperm cell in the female's body during intercourse, a baby may be conceived. Also called an ovum.

ejaculation (ee-JACK-you-lay-shun). The spurting of semen or sperm from a man's penis, which usually occurs at the climax of sexual intercourse or other type of stimulation.

ejaculatory ducts (ee-JACK-yuh-la-tor-ee ducts). Canals in the male formed by the intersection of the vas deferens and the duct from the seminal vesicle. They pass through the prostate. Semen travels through them at the time of ejaculation.

embryo (EM-bree-oh). The fourth stage in the development of a baby inside the mother's body. This is the term for the development stage that starts about fourteen days after the sperm fertilizes the ovum (egg), and continues until the eighth week of pregnancy. After that, it is called a fetus.

emergency contraceptive pill (emergency con-tra-SEP-tiv pill) or **ECP.** A pill a female can take after having sex to prevent pregnancy. The pill is effective when taken immediately after having sex or up to three to five days later. Also called "morning-after pill."

emotions (ee-MOE-shuns). Moods and feelings, ranging from extreme happiness to extreme sadness or anger, which are particularly pronounced during adolescence because of hormonal changes.

endometrium (en-doe-MEE-tree-um). The velvety lining of the uterus, where a fertilized egg develops.

epididymis (ep-ih-DID-ih-mus). Tiny tubes located behind each testicle in which sperm cells mature.

epidural block (ep-ih-DUR-al block). A form of local anesthesia administered to the lower portion of the mother's body during childbirth to reduce pain.

episiotomy (ee-pee-zee-AH-tah-mee). A surgical incision a doctor makes in the mother from her vagina to the perineum at the time of birth. This is sometimes necessary to allow the baby to pass through the vagina more easily.

erectile dysfunction (ee-RECK-tul dis-FUNK-shun) or **ED.** *See* impotent.

erectile dysfunction (ED) drugs. Prescription drugs that enable a man to achieve and maintain an erection.

erection (ee-RECK-shun). The enlargement and hardening of a man's penis, which makes sexual intercourse possible. It is usually caused by sexual arousal.

erotic (ee-RAH-tic). Meant to or tending to arouse sexual desire or strongly affected by sexual desire.

estrogen (ESS-tro-jen). The female sex hormone produced in the ovaries. It affects the menstrual cycle and the development of a woman's sexual characteristics. Production of the hormone increases during puberty, resulting in the growth of breasts, pubic hair, and other changes.

F

Fallopian tubes (fah-LOW-pee-an tubes). The part of a female's sex organs through which the egg cells pass from the ovaries to the uterus. The egg cell and sperm cell meet in a Fallopian tube when conception occurs. The fertilized egg cell then moves to the uterus. Also called oviducts.

false labor. Pains a pregnant woman may experience that are not actual labor pains. Also called Braxton Hicks contractions.

family planning. The decisions parents make about how many children to have and when they would like to have them.

fantasize. To daydream or think about things that you want to happen or that you would enjoy, including sexual things. People often fantasize while masturbating as well as other times.

father. The male partner who, along with the mother, brings children into the world.

female (FEE-male). A girl or woman.

female athletic syndrome or **female athlete triad.** A phenomenon whereby a female who engages in extremely strenuous sports training develops three problems: eating disorders, amenorrhea (delay in first menstruation or interruption of normal menstrual cycles), and bone problems that can lead to early osteoporosis (brittle bones).

female condom (female CON-dum). A barrier method of contraceptive in which a hollow tube with one closed end is placed into the vagina. Whereas the male condom covers the outside of the penis, the female condom covers the inside of the vagina. It prevents pregnancy and disease.

fertile (FUR-till). Physically able to produce children.

fertile mucus (FUR-till MYOO-kus). A thick vaginal discharge that is released around the time the female ovulates. This mucus nourishes the male's sperm and allows it to pass freely through the female's cervix, thereby increasing the female's chances of getting pregnant.

fertility (fur-TIL-ih-tee). The state of being fertile.

fertility awareness method. A practice in which a woman monitors one or more of her primary fertility signs to determine the fertile and infertile times of her menstrual cycle. Women may do this to prevent pregnancy (by not having sex when fertile) or to achieve pregnancy (by having sex when fertile). It is not considered to be an effective way to prevent pregnancy. *See also* calendar method; ovulation method; temperature method.

fertilization (fur-till-eye-ZA-shun). The meeting of a sperm cell and an egg cell.

fetal alcohol syndrome (FEE-tahl alcohol syndrome). A serious, lifelong disorder in babies born to mothers who drink alcohol heavily while they are pregnant. It causes developmental disabilities and deformities.

fetoscopy (fee-TAH-scop-ee). Direct examination of the fetus using a fetoscope or thin tube containing a scope.

fetus (FEE-tus). The fifth stage in the development of a baby inside the mother's body. This is the term for the development stage that starts in the eighth week of pregnancy and lasts until birth.

fimbriae (FIM-bree-ee). The fringe at the end of each Fallopian tube that help draw an egg cell into the tube on its way to the uterus.

follicle-stimulating hormone (FALL-ick-el STIM-you-late-ing HOR-moan) or **FSH.** A hormone produced by the pituitary gland in both males and females. FSH causes either the female egg follicle or the male sperm follicle to mature.

follicles (FALL-ick-els). Small sacs that contain egg cells in a female. Also refers to male sperm follicles.

fontanel (fon-ton-ELL). The membrane-covered soft spot in a newborn baby's head, which closes a few weeks after birth.

food addiction (food ah-DICK-shun). An intense need to eat, even when not really hungry. Food addicts crave food, think about it all the time, and usually feel guilty about what they eat.

foreplay (FOR-play). The kissing and touching that take place before intercourse.

foreskin (FOR-skin). The skin covering the tip of the penis. This skin is removed when a boy is circumcised. *See* prepuce (1).

formula. Specially prepared liquid that substitutes for a mother's breast milk. Some babies are fed only formula; others breastfeed and also drink some formula.

fornication (for-nih-KAY-shun). Sexual relations between unmarried people.

fraternal twins (frah-TER-nal twins). Twins produced by two egg cells meeting with two sperm cells. *See also* identical twins; twins.

French kiss. A romantic, passionate kiss in which the tongue enters the partner's mouth. Also referred to as a tongue kiss.

frenulum (FREN-ya-lum). The Y-shaped connecting tissue on the underside of the glans of the penis. It has many nerve endings and is very sensitive. Most of it is usually removed when a boy is circumcised.

G

gay. *See* homosexual.

gender (JEN-der). Sex; either male or female.

gender identity (JEN-der eye-DEN-tih-tee). A person's sense of being either a male or female. Sometimes a person with the body of one gender may feel that he or she is really the opposite gender. *See also* transgender.

genes (JEENZ). The tiny units of heredity carried by the chromosomes.

genetic counseling. The application of what is known about human genetics to problems that may arise during a pregnancy.

genetics (jen-ETT-icks). The science of heredity. How traits are passed by the genes from one generation to another.

genital herpes (JEN-ih-tal HER-peez). A type of viral sexually transmitted disease that produces sores on the sex organs.

genital warts (JEN-ih-tal warts). A type of viral sexually transmitted disease that produces small warts on and around the sex organs.

genitalia (JEN-ih-TALE-ya). *See* genitals.

genitals (JEN-ih-tals). Usually refers to the external sexual organs of a male or a female. Also called genitalia.

gestation (jes-TAY-shun). The nine-month period during which a baby develops inside its mother's uterus.

gestational diabetes (jes-TAY-shun-uhl DIE-uh-BEET-eez). A type of diabetes that occurs only during pregnancy. It is characterized by dangerously high blood sugar levels, which typically return to normal soon after the woman delivers her baby.

glands. Organs in the body that make hormones or other substances (including breast milk).

glans (glanz). In a male, the extreme end, or head, of the penis. In a female, the tip of the clitoris.

gonococcus (gone-oh-KAH-kus). A germ that causes gonorrhea.

gonorrhea (gone-oh-REE-ah). A common and serious sexually transmitted disease caused by bacteria that can grow and multiply easily in the warm, moist areas of the reproductive system.

groin (groyn). The part of the body where the legs join with the torso, around the pubic area.

growth spurt. Refers to a period in a girl's or boy's life when she or he suddenly grows taller and begins to develop rapidly.

gynecological exam (guy-nah-co-LODGE-ih-kal exam). Examination by a doctor of a woman's external genitals as well as the vagina and cervix.

gynecologist (guy-nah-CALL-oh-jist). A doctor who specializes in all areas of female medicine.

gynecology (guy-nah-CALL-oh-gee). The branch of medicine that deals with the diseases and hygiene of women.

gynecomastia (GUY-nah-kuh-MAS-tee-ah). Excessive development of male breasts. Temporary enlargement of the breasts is not unusual or abnormal in boys during adolescence, and it usually disappears within two years.

H

hemorrhoids (HEM-or-oids). A mass of swollen, dilated veins near or inside the anal opening caused by straining to have a bowel movement. Hemorrhoids also may occur due to the pushing a woman exerts when giving birth to a child.

hepatitis (HEP-uh-tie-tus). A virus that attacks the liver. It occurs in different forms, designated by A, B, C, D, and E, and can be transmitted through poor hygiene, sex, needles, or from an infected mother to her unborn baby. Some forms of the virus can be transmitted in other ways as well.

heredity (her-ED-ih-tee). The characteristics parents pass to their children through the genes.

herpes (HER-peez). Viral diseases of the skin. Some, but not all, are sexually transmitted. *See also* genital herpes.

heterosexual (het-er-oh-SEKS-you-uhl). A person who is sexually attracted only to people of the opposite sex.

homophobia (hoe-moe-FOE-bee-ah). Fear of homosexuals and homosexuality.

homosexual (hoe-moe-SEKS-you-uhl). A person who is sexually attracted only to people of the same sex. Also referred to as gay.

hormones (HOR-moans). Chemicals secreted by the glands, some of which produce sexual differences between men and women.

human chorionic gonadotropin (human KOR-ee-ahn-ick GO-nad-uh-TRO-pin) or **HCG**. A hormone that is produced during pregnancy. This is the hormone that is detected by pregnancy tests to determine whether a female is pregnant.

human immunodeficiency virus (human im-YOU-no-de-FISH-en-see virus) or **HIV.** A virus that can lead to acquired immunodeficiency syndrome (AIDS), which causes the immune system to fail. It can be transmitted through sex, needles, or from an infected mother to her unborn baby.

human papillomavirus (human pap-il-OH-ma-VI-rus) or **HPV.** A group of viruses that includes more than 100 different types. More than thirty of these viruses are sexually transmitted and can infect the genital area of men and women.

human papillomavirus (HPV) vaccine (human pap-il-OH-ma-VI-rus VAK-seen). Approved by the U.S. Food and Drug Administration (FDA) in 2006, this vaccine, called Gardasil®, protects against four HPV types, which together cause 70 percent of cervical cancers and 90 percent of genital warts. It is approved for use in females ages nine to twenty-six. Studies are being done to determine whether the vaccine would also work for males.

husband. The male partner in a marriage.

hygiene (HIGH-jeen). Keeping the body parts clean and healthy.

hymen (HIGH-men). A layer of tissue (or membrane) covering or partially covering the opening of the vagina. It may be broken by intercourse, surgical incision, the use of tampons, or even strenuous exercise.

I

identical twins (eye-DEN-tick-al twins). Two babies that are started by the same fertilized egg, which then divides into two parts. *See also* fraternal twins; twins

immoral (im-MORE-al). Going against commonly held moral principles; sometimes refers to being unchaste or having sexual relations before marriage.

immune system. The body's defense system against disease. When a person has AIDS, the immune system cannot combat infections.

implantation (im-plant-TA-shun). The process in which a blastocyst attaches itself to the mother's uterine wall. There it develops into an embryo and then a fetus.

impotent (IM-pet-ent). Lacking power or strength. In sexual terms, it refers to a man's being unable to achieve or maintain an erection of the penis. The cause may be physiological or psychological. Also called erectile dysfunction.

in vitro fertilization (in-VEE-tro fer-tuhl-uh-ZAY-shun). Fertilization of an egg cell by a sperm cell outside a woman's body under laboratory conditions. The fertilized egg cell is then inserted into the uterus.

incest (IN-sest). Sexual intercourse between people who are so closely related they are forbidden by law to marry each other, such as between a father and daughter or between a brother and sister.

infant. Baby.

infatuation (in-FAT-u-ay-shun). A foolish or extravagant love or affection for another person.

infertility (in-fer-TILL-i-tee). The inability to produce children. Either a man or a woman may be infertile.

inguinal hernia (ING-gwuh-nuhl HER-nee-uh). A type of hernia that occurs in a male's lower abdomen, causing pain and a bulge in the scrotum. An operation is usually necessary to repair the condition.

inherited traits. Physical and other features that parents pass on to their children, such as height, weight, intelligence, and sense of humor.

intercourse (IN-ter-kors). Can mean any interaction or communication. In sexual terms, it usually refers to the mating of a man and a woman. This involves the insertion of a man's penis into a woman's vagina and is called vaginal intercourse. During vaginal intercourse a baby may be, but is not always, conceived.

intimate (IN-tih-mit). Very personal or private. Intimate relations sometimes refers to sexual relations between a man and a woman.

intrauterine device (in-truh-YOU-ter-in device) or **IUD.** A metal or plastic birth control device that a doctor can place in a woman's uterus through the vagina.

IUD. *See* intrauterine device.

J

jealous (JEL-uhs). Being fearful of losing another person's love or affection.

K

kinky (KING-kee). Appealing to strange or unusual tastes, especially in regard to sexual matters.

kiss. To caress or touch with the lips to express affection.

L

labia (LAY-bee-eh). The folds of skin, or "lips," on the external female genitals surrounding the vaginal opening. There is an outer part (labia majora) and an inner part (labia minora).

labia majora (LAY-bee-eh meh-JOR-eh). The outer lips surrounding the vaginal opening.

labia minora (LAY-bee-eh meh-NOR-eh). The inner lips surrounding the vaginal opening.

labor. The effort a mother puts forth during childbirth. During this process, the uterus has contractions, which help to push the baby out, and the cervix dilates (opens) to allow the baby to leave the uterus.

lactational amenorrhea method (lack-TAY-shun-al a-MEN-uh-REE-uh method). A method of birth control based on the idea that a woman who is nursing is less likely to ovulate for six months after a baby is born. It is not considered an effective way to prevent pregnancy.

lactogenesis (lack-toe-GEN-eh-sis). When milk production begins in a mother's breasts shortly after birth.

Lamaze (lah-MAHZ). A method of childbirth involving the physical and psychological preparation of the mother. It helps suppress pain and often allows the mother to deliver the baby without the use of drugs.

larynx (LAIR-inks). An organ in the neck that produces sound. During adolescence, a boy's larynx may become much larger. In men, the bulge of the larynx on the outside of the neck is called the Adam's apple.

Leboyer method (Lah-BOY-er method). A natural childbirth method developed by Frederick Leboyer, M.D. The newborn baby is delivered in a quiet, dimly lit room and placed immediately on its mother's abdomen. Then the baby is placed in warm water and rocked gently.

legal age. The age at which a person is considered competent (by law) to have sexual intercourse or other sexual activity. The legal age is different, depending on the state.

lesbian (LEZ-bee-un). A female homosexual.

love. The powerful emotional force that draws people together. Physical love between a man and a woman often results in the birth of a new human being.

lubrication (LOOB-ruh-KAY-shun). The act of producing or applying a wet, slippery substance to reduce friction and allow for smooth movements. When aroused, the female and male sex organs produce a lubricating mucus to allow the penis to easily enter the vagina during sex.

lymphoceles (LIMF-oh-seels). An appearance of firm, veinlike swellings on the penis, which can occur after injury or vigorous sexual stimulation, but also sometimes for no apparent reason. The swelling is caused by a blockage of the lymph glands near the corona and usually disappears in a few weeks without treatment.

M

maidenhead. Refers to the hymen. Also refers to being a maiden or virgin. *See* hymen.

making out. Kissing, hugging, and touching in a sexual way with a partner. *See also* necking; petting.

male. A boy or man.

mammary glands. Another name for female breasts.

marriage (MARE-ij). The state of being married; the legal union of a husband and wife usually for the purpose of founding and maintaining a family.

masturbation (mass-tur-BAY-shun). Self-stimulation of the sex organs.

mate. A spouse or close companion.

maternal (ma-TER-nal). Having to do with a mother.

menarche (MEN-ar-kee). A girl's first menstrual period.

menopause (MEN-oh-pahz). A time in a woman's life when the ovaries stop producing egg cells and hormones, and menstruation ceases. It is sometimes called the "change of life."

menstrual cramps (MEN-stroo-al cramps). The painful feelings some females experience in their lower abdomens during their menstrual periods.

menstrual cycle (MEN-stroo-al cycle). The monthly fertility cycle most women experience beginning with the first day of menstruation and continuing for about a month until the next cycle begins.

menstrual period (MEN-stroo-al period). Normally, the three- to six-day period when menstruation takes place. A girl can begin having menstrual periods as early as age eight, and usually no later than age sixteen. Also referred to as period.

menstruation (MEN-stroo-AY-shun). The monthly discharge of blood from a female's uterus. Menstruation occurs approximately every 28 days. If a baby is conceived, menstruation stops during the nine-month pregnancy period and then resumes again after the baby is born.

midwife. A nonphysician health care practitioner who is trained to take care of a woman and her baby during pregnancy, childbirth, and the postpartum period.

milk. The nourishing liquid produced by a mother's breasts following the birth of a baby.

miscarriage (MIS-care-ij). The loss of an embryo from the uterus, especially during the first three months of pregnancy.

molest (moh-LEST). To sexually abuse or harm someone, usually a child.

molester (moh-LESS-ter). Someone who sexually abuses or harms another person, usually a child.

monogamy (mah-NOG-ah-me). Marrying only once during a lifetime or having only one marriage partner at a time.

mons pubis (mons PYOO-bis). In females, the rounded, soft area above the pubic bone. Also referred to as mons veneris.

mons veneris (mons VEN-ur-is). *See* mons pubis.

mood swings. Emotional highs and lows that change quickly. Adolescents often have mood swings, when they may feel wonderful one moment and just awful a few minutes later. These mood swings are made greater by hormone changes in the body.

morality (more-AL-ih-tee). Living by high moral principles—sometimes refers to being chaste or not having sexual intercourse before marriage.

morning sickness. Nausea and vomiting experienced by many pregnant women, caused by the surge of hormones in the woman's body. Although it commonly occurs in the morning during the first trimester, it can happen at any time of day and can continue throughout the pregnancy.

morning-after pill. *See* emergency contraceptive pill.

morula (MOR-ya-lah). The second stage in the development of a baby inside the mother's body. This is the term for the development stage that starts about thirty hours after the sperm fertilizes the ovum (egg), and continues until about the fourth day.

mother. The female partner who, along with a father, brings children into the world.

mucus (MYOO-kus). A sticky substance produced by various body parts, including a female's cervix and a male's Cowper's glands.

mutual masturbation (MYOO-chew-all mass-tur-BAY-shun). Sexual activity in which two people touch each other and come to orgasm, without penetration.

N

natural birth control or **natural family planning.** *See* fertility awareness method.

natural childbirth. To give birth without receiving anesthesia.

nausea (NAH-zee-ah or NAH-zha). Feeling sick to the stomach. *See* morning sickness.

navel. *See* belly button.

necking. A term used to describe a couple sitting close together, kissing, and touching one another for the purposes of sexual pleasure. *See also* making out; petting.

newborn. A newly born baby.

nipple. The small protuberance on each side of the male's chest and at the tips of the female's breasts. It can be a sexually sensitive area for both the male and female. For the breastfeeding mother, the nipple performs the same function as the nipple on a baby bottle. The baby sucks on it and nurses or draws milk from its mother.

nocturnal emission (nock-TURN-uhl ee-MISH-un). The release of sperm while sleeping. This happens occasionally, usually beginning around the age of thirteen. Also called "wet dream."

nongonococcal urethritis (nahn-gahn-uh-KAH-kul yer-eh-THRY-tus) or **NGU.** A sexually transmitted disease (not gonorrhea).

noninsertive sex. *See* outercourse.

nonoxynol-9 (non-OX-i-nol nine). A spermicide used in contraceptive products. May be in cream, foam, or jelly form. It was once thought to reduce the risk of sexually transmitted diseases, but recent studies show that it does not.

nurse. To draw nourishment from a mother's breast. *See* breastfeeding.

O

obesity (Oh-BEE-sit-ee). Being so overweight that it can be unhealthy. Obesity is associated with heart disease, diabetes, some kinds of cancer, and arthritis.

obstetrician (ob-sta-TRIH-shun). A doctor who takes care of a woman and her baby during pregnancy, childbirth, and the postpartum period.

oral intercourse (OR-ul IN-ter-kors) or **oral sex** (OR-ul seks). The placement of the mouth on the genitals of another person for sexual stimulation.

orchidometer (or-kih-DOM-uh-ter). An instrument used to measure the volume of testicles. Doctors monitor the size of testicles because abnormal size can be a sign of certain diseases or maturation problems.

orgasm (OR-gaz-um). The climax of sexual pleasure during intercourse or other stimulation of the sex organs.

os (ohs). The opening of the uterus.

osteoporosis (ah-stee-oh-por-OH-sis). A disease that causes bones to become brittle and more likely to break. A person who does not have enough calcium in his or her diet during puberty is more likely to develop this disease when he or she is older. It affects both sexes, but women are four times more likely to develop the disease.

outercourse. To sexually stimulate a partner without engaging in intercourse. This may be done to prevent pregnancy and sexually transmitted disease. A couple may also choose to engage in only this type of sexual activity because they don't feel ready to have intercourse. Also called noninsertive sex.

ova (OH-vah). Egg cells in the female. Plural of ovum. *See also* egg cell.

ovarian cyst (oh-VAR-ee-an sist). An abnormal growth on the ovary.

ovarian follicles (oh-VAR-ee-an FALL-ick-els). Small spheres inside the ovaries, each containing one ovum.

ovaries (OH-vah-reez). Plural of ovary.

ovary (OH-vah-ree). The organ in the female where egg cells and sex hormones are produced and stored.

oviducts (OH-vah-ducts). *See* Fallopian tube.

ovulation (ahv-you-LAY-shun). The release of an egg cell from the ovary, which occurs in a female about once a month. Ovulation may begin as early as age eight. The egg cell travels through the Fallopian tube to the uterus. There, it is either fertilized by a sperm cell or expelled through menstruation.

ovulation method (ahv-you-LAY-shun method). A fertility awareness method in which a female examines her vaginal discharge of cervical mucus to determine whether she is ovulating. *See also* fertility awareness method.

ovum (OH-vum). *See* egg cell.

P

pad. A long, narrow cotton material that is placed in a female's undergarment to absorb blood during menstruation. Also called a sanitary napkin.

Pap test or **Pap smear.** A routine test performed in a doctor's office to test for cancer of the cervix.

paracervical block (para-SERV-ick-al block). A local anesthetic injected near the cervix (or neck of the uterus) to reduce pain during labor.

parenting. The skills used by a mother and father in bearing and rearing children.

parturition (par-chur-IH-shun). The action or process of giving birth to offspring. *See also* labor.

passion (PASH-un). An extremely compelling emotion; can refer to love or anger.

paternal (pa-TER-nal). Having to do with a father.

pearly penile papules (PER-lee PEE-nile PAP-yules). Small, dome-shaped bumps around the corona of the penis. The cause of the condition, which is harmless and does not need treatment, is unknown. When the bumps appear during puberty or adolescence, they often disappear over time.

peer pressure. When a person or group encourages a person of the same age to do something—such as have sex, take drugs, or drink alcohol—that the person doesn't want to do or that could get the person into trouble. This commonly refers to young people in their preteen and teenage years.

pelvic exam (PEL-vik exam). A doctor's examination of a female's reproductive system to determine whether any health problems, such as cancer, sexually transmitted diseases, or infections, are present in the area. It is usually performed by a female's primary care physician or gynecologist.

pelvic inflammatory disease (PEL-vik in-FLAM-ah-tory disease) or **PID.** A bacteria-caused infection that travels from the vagina or cervix to the uterus and Fallopian tubes. It can cause infertility.

pelvis (PEL-vis). The basin-shaped structure in the middle of the body, formed by the hip bones on the sides, pubic bone in front, and tail bone in back.

penetration (pen-eh-TRAY-shun). When part of one person's body is put into an opening in another person's body. One kind of penetration is a man's penis entering a woman's vagina. But penetration can include tongues or fingers or objects being put into the mouth, anus, or vagina.

penis (PEE-nuhs). The major male sex organ. *See* sex organs.

penis shaft (PEE-nuhs shaft). The main length of the penis made up of erectile tissue covered by skin.

performance anxiety (per-FOR-mints ANG-zy-a-tee). A male's fear that he will not be able to achieve an erection during a sexual encounter. The fear sometimes prevents an erection.

perinatal (pair-ih-NAY-tal). Pertaining to or occurring during the period shortly before or shortly after birth.

perineum (pare-eh-NEE-em). Usually refers to the area of the female anatomy located between the vagina and the anus. Also refers to the area of the male anatomy located between the scrotum and the anus.

period. *See* menstrual period.

perspiration (per-spur-AY-shun). Sweat. When the body gives off fluid to help keep it cool. Perspiration is heavier under the arms, but humans sweat over almost all of their bodies.

pervert (PUR-vert). A person who commits unnatural sexual acts.

petting. Touching someone else's body to arouse sexual pleasure.

physical traits. Characteristics in a person's appearance that are inherited from his or her parents, such as eye color, hair color, height, and weight.

pill, the. *See* birth control pills.

pimples (PIM-puhlz). Small, inflamed spots on the skin common in boys and girls of adolescent age. Also called acne or zits.

pituitary gland (pih-TOO-ah-tair-ee gland). A tiny gland at the base of the brain that controls the other glands in the body. During adolescence it begins the process of changing a girl into a young woman and a boy into a young man.

placenta (pluh-CENT-ah). A temporary, waffle-shaped organ that exchanges nutrients and wastes between the mother and the fetus. The placenta also produces hormones necessary to maintain pregnancy. *See also* afterbirth.

PMS. *See* premenstrual syndrome.

polygamy (pah-LIG-ah-me). Marriage in which the male may have more than one wife or the female may have more than one husband.

pornography (por-NAH-gra-fee). Books, magazines, videos, and other material that show or describe erotic activities for the purpose of sexual excitement.

postpartum (post-PAR-tum). The time following the birth of a child.

postpartum depression (post-PAR-tum depression). A period of depression some women experience for several weeks after the birth of a child. It is believed to be caused primarily by sudden hormonal changes that occur in a woman's body after giving birth. Stress, lack of sleep, and other factors may also contribute to depression. Also referred to as "baby blues."

preeclampsia (PRE-uh-CLAMP-see-uh). *See* toxemia.

pre-ejaculatory fluid (pre-ee-JACK-yuh-la-tor-ee FLU-id). Mucus produced by the Cowper's glands before a male ejaculates. It serves to lubricate the end of the penis before intercourse and to protect sperm as it passes through the male's urethra.

preemie. *See* premature baby.

pregnancy. The nine-month period following conception when a baby develops inside its mother's uterus.

pregnancy-induced hypertension. *See* toxemia.

pregnant. Refers to a woman who is carrying an unborn child inside her uterus.

premarital intercourse (pree-MARE-it-al IN-ter-kors) or **premarital sex** (pree-MARE-it-al seks). Having sexual relations before marriage.

premature baby. A baby born before the full nine months of the mother's pregnancy, usually weighing under five pounds.

premenstrual syndrome (PREE-men-stroo-al syndrome) or **PMS.** A phenomenon in which a female experiences unpleasant symptoms, including headaches, bloating, cramps, and irritability, a few days before getting her monthly menstrual period.

prenatal (pre-NAY-tuhl). The time or period before birth.

prenatal care (pre-NAY-tal care). The health care given to a mother during her pregnancy.

prepuce (PRE-pyoos). Can refer either to (1) the foreskin of a male's penis or (2) a similar fold of skin covering a female's clitoris. On the female, it is also referred to as the clitoral hood. *See also* clitoral hood; foreskin.

prescription drugs. Medications that are available only when ordered by a doctor.

preventive behavior. Behavior that gives at least some protection against spreading sexually transmitted diseases.

pro-choice. The belief that a pregnant woman should have the right to choose whether to have an abortion.

progesterone (pro-JESS-ter-ohn). The female sex hormone, which prepares a woman's uterus to receive and sustain a fertilized egg. It is sometimes called the "pregnancy hormone." It also causes a mother's breasts to produce milk for a newborn baby.

prolapsed cord (PRO-lapst cord). An umbilical cord that has wrapped around the unborn baby's neck and is restricting blood flow to the baby. This endangers the baby's life during childbirth and may require a doctor to deliver the baby by Cesarean section.

pro-life. The belief that abortion should be illegal because it is the taking of human life.

promiscuous (pro-MIS-cue-us). Behavior in which a person randomly and casually engages in sexual activity, usually with several different partners over the course of a short period of time.

prostaglandin (PRAHS-tuh-GLAN-dun). A chemical the female body releases when the uterus sheds its lining each month during the menstrual period. It causes the uterus to contract, which is the reason some women experience cramping.

prostate gland (prah-state gland). A gland surrounding the male urethra. From it comes a milky fluid that is part of the semen. The muscles around the urethra are the main source of ejaculation.

prostatitis (pros-tah-TITE-us). Inflammation of the prostate.

puberty (PYOO-ber-tee). The years between approximately ages ten and thirteen when girls begin to change into young women and boys begin to change into young men. These changes happen at different times for every boy and girl. *See also* adolescence.

pubic hair (PYOO-bic hair). Hair surrounding the sexual organs of a girl or a boy. This hair develops during adolescence.

pubic lice. *See* crabs.

pudendum (pyoo-DEN-dum). The external sexual organs of a human being, especially of a woman.

pullout method. *See* coitus interruptus.

purge. When talking about an eating disorder, a purge is inducing vomiting to get rid of food that has just been eaten.

Q

quickening. The time during a mother's pregnancy when she first begins to feel the movement of the baby in the uterus. It usually occurs about the fourth or fifth month.

R

rape. The crime of sexual intercourse without one of the participant's consent and usually by force.

raphe (RAY-fee). A continuous ridge of tissue that creates a line. It is found in various parts of the body, including one on the male reproductive organs, which extends from the anus through the middle of the scrotum and up through the middle of the underside of the penis.

recessive trait (re-SESS-iv trait). A trait that is not dominant. *See* dominant trait.

reproduction (ree-pro-DUK-shun). The process of having children or "reproducing" human life.

reproductive organs (ree-pro-DUK-tive OR-gunz). The organs in the body of a male or female that have to do with producing children. Also referred to as reproductive system and sex organs. *See also* sex organs.

retractile testicles (ree-TRACK-tuhl TES-tick-uhls). A condition in which one or both of a young boy's testicles pulls up to the top of the scrotum or into the body from time to time. It usually corrects itself by the time the boy reaches puberty but if it doesn't, it may need to be surgically corrected.

Rh incompatibility (R-H in-come-pat-ih-BIL-it-ee). This happens when a mother has Rh-negative blood and her baby has Rh-positive, or vice versa. The mother's blood produces antibodies that may endanger the fetuses of future pregnancies. Injections of gamma globulin may be given to the mother to prevent her body from producing these antibodies.

rhythm method (RIH-them method). *See* fertility awareness method.

risky behavior. Behavior that may lead to a sexually transmitted disease such as AIDS.

romance (ro-MANS). Love or passion.

romantic love. An intimate or passionate love.

rubber. *See* condom.

S

saddle block. A type of anesthesia given by injection into the mother's lower spinal area to block her pain during labor and delivery.

safe behavior. Behavior that prevents sexually transmitted diseases.

safe sex or **safer sex.** Sexual activity that is unlikely to expose a person to AIDS or other sexually transmitted diseases. No body fluids are shared. Examples include using a condom during intercourse, and engaging only in outercourse.

sanitary napkin. *See* pad.

scrotum (SKRO-tum). The sac under the penis containing the testicles.

sebaceous glands (see-BAY-shus glands). Glands that secrete an oily material under the skin. These glands are particularly active during adolescence.

sebum (SEE-bem). Fatty lubricant matter secreted by the sebaceous glands of the skin. Sometimes associated with acne.

secondary sexual characteristics (SEC-un-dare-ee SEKS-you-uhl CARE-ick-ter-IS-ticks). The changes that occur in a young person's body during adolescence, such as the development of hair under the arms, pubic hair, a deepening voice in boys, and developing breasts in girls.

seed. Sometimes refers to sperm cells. *See* sperm.

self-control. In a sexual sense, acting responsibly and not giving in to impulsive actions. *See also* safe behavior.

semen (SEE-mun). The thick, white fluid that contains sperm and is ejaculated from the penis.

seminal vesicles (SEM-in-al VESS-ick-als). Two sacs where semen is stored. They are located near the prostate.

seminiferous tubules (sem-i-NIF-er-us TU-byuls). Structures located in the testes that produce sperm.

sex (seks). Male or female. Also refers to sexual intercourse. *See also* gender; intercourse.

sex organs (seks OR-gunz). The organs that are part of the reproductive system. The major sex organ for a boy is his penis; for a girl, her vagina. *See also* reproductive organs.

sex role (seks role). The way a society indicates how a man or woman ought to behave. Also refers to what is expected of a mother or father.

sexual characteristics (SEK-shoo-uhl CARE-ick-ter-IS-ticks). Those characteristics that distinguish a man from a woman. *See also* secondary sexual characteristics.

sexual intercourse (SEK-shoo-uhl IN-ter-kors). *See* intercourse.

sexual intimacy (SEK-shoo-uhl IN-tih-muh-see). The expression of physical feeling through sexual behavior.

sexual orientation (SEK-shoo-uhl OR-ee-en-TAY-shun). Refers to a person's sexual preference in terms of whether he or she is bisexual (attracted to both sexes), heterosexual (attracted to people of the opposite sex), or homosexual (attracted to people of the same sex).

sexuality (SEK-shoo-AL-uh-tee). A person's sexual nature; having to do with being male or female. Also refers to sexual behavior.

sexually active (SEK-shoo-uhl-ee active). Taking part in sexual activities, usually used to mean having sexual intercourse as part of those activities.

sexually transmitted diseases (SEK-shoo-uhl-ee transmitted diseases) (**STDs**). Diseases that may result from sexual intercourse or other intimate contact. Also called venereal diseases.

sexy. Sexually attractive or interesting.

shaft. *See* penis shaft.

shield, the. A barrier method of contraception in which a soft silicone cup fits snugly over the cervix to block sperm from entering. It is used with spermicide to prevent pregnancy.

Siamese twins (SIE-uh-MEEZ twins). *See* conjoined twins.

Skene's glands (skeens glands). Two small glands located in the vagina near the lower end of the urethra. Some experts believe that the glands produce a fluid that is ejaculated during a woman's orgasm.

smegma (SMEG-mah). A thick, white substance that collects under the foreskin of a uncircumcised boy, if the foreskin is not pulled back and cleaned. This substance can cause odor and irritation. It can also collect under the foreskin of a girl's clitoris. These areas need to be cleaned daily with soap and water.

sodomy (SAW-duh-mee). The act of having anal or oral intercourse, or intercourse with an animal. The word comes from the biblical story of Sodom.

speculum (SPEK-you-lum). A medical instrument used to hold open the walls of the vagina during a pelvic exam and Pap smear.

sperm or **sperm cell.** The male reproductive cell. When a sperm cell meets with an egg cell in the female's body during intercourse, a baby may be conceived.

spermatozoa (sper-MA-tah-ZOE-uh). The scientific name for sperm cells.

spermicide (SPER-ma-side). A substance that kills sperm cells and is used to help prevent pregnancy.

spirochetes (SPY-ro-keets). Slender corkscrew-shaped bacteria that cause syphilis.

spontaneous erection (spontaneous ee-RECK-shun). When a male gets an erection without having any sexual feelings or thoughts. This commonly happens to boys during puberty because of the hormonal increases their bodies are experiencing.

spotting. Small amounts of vaginal bleeding that may occur between a female's menstrual periods. This is a common side effect of many types of contraceptives that use hormones.

spouse. A marriage partner, either male or female.

statutory rape. A criminal act that happens when an adult has sex with a minor, even if the minor agreed to engage in sex. Under the law, a minor is not considered capable of making a responsible decision regarding whether to have sex.

sterility (ster-ILL-eh-tee). Being sterile or unable to have children.

sterilization (stare-ill-eye-ZAY-shun). A surgical procedure that prevents a man from impregnating a woman or a woman from becoming pregnant.

stillbirth. When a fetus that has died in the mother's womb, or during labor or delivery, is expelled or removed from the woman's body.

straight. *See* heterosexual.

stretch marks. Lines that can appear when a part of the body, such as a female's breasts, grows. Women may also experience stretch marks on the abdomen as a result of pregnancy.

sweat glands (swet glands). Glands, particularly under the arms, that become more active during adolescence. Greater body odor is normal as a young person matures, and greater effort is needed to keep the body clean.

sympathetic pregnancy. *See* couvade syndrome.

syphilis (SIH-fill-iss). A serious but curable sexually transmitted disease.

T

tampon (TAM-pahn). A small roll of absorbent cotton a female inserts into her vagina to absorb menstrual flow.

T-cells. Another name for T-lymphocytes, also known as white blood cells. HIV destroys these cells. A healthy person has one thousand to two thousand T-cells per cubic millimeter of blood. A person who has HIV is considered to have AIDS when his or her T-cells are down to about two hundred per cubic millimeter of blood.

temperature method. A fertility awareness method of birth control where the female takes her basal body temperature each day to determine whether she is ovulating. *See also* fertility awareness method.

teratogen (teh-RAT-eh-jen). Any agent that might interfere with the normal development of a fetus and result in the loss of a pregnancy, a birth defect, or a pregnancy complication. Teratogens could be in the form of medications, alcohol, cigarettes, infectious diseases, chemicals in the environment, or other agents.

test tube baby. A baby conceived by in vitro fertilization.

testes (TES-teez). A plural form of testicle. *See* testicles.

testicles (TES-tick-uhlz). Two oval-shaped glands, which produce sperm cells. They are located inside the scrotum.

testicular self-examination (tes-TIC-u-lar self-examination) or **TSE.** A technique for examining the testicles for lumps or other abnormalities. The purpose of this is to detect testicular cancer in its earliest stages, when it is more likely to be successfully treated.

testosterone (tes-TOSS-ter-ohn). A hormone, produced in the testicles, that affects the development of male sexual characteristics. Production of the hormone increases during puberty, resulting in growth of muscles, facial and body hair, sperm production, and other changes.

tongue kiss. *See* French kiss.

toxemia (tocks-EE-me-uh). A serious condition a woman can develop during pregnancy in which she has high blood pressure, severe edema (swelling), and protein in her urine. It can result in the death of the mother or fetus if not controlled. Also referred to as preeclampsia or pregnancy-induced hypertension.

toxic shock syndrome (TSS). A rare condition affecting both males and females, and caused by staph bacteria. Females who use tampons have a slight risk of contracting TSS. If tampons are not changed frequently enough, it allows the bacteria in the blood to multiply, leading to the condition. Symptoms include fever, vomiting, and diarrhea; the condition can be fatal.

traditional family. Generally used to mean a family that consists of a married man and woman with children.

transgender (TRANZ-JEN-der). A person who feels he or she is the opposite gender, or who does not identify with either gender, female or male.

transmitted (trans-MIH-ted). Something that is spread or passed along. In the context of disease, transmission refers to passing something from one person to another.

trichomoniasis (trik-oh-moe-NYE-uh-sis). A common sexually transmitted disease. It mostly affects women, whose symptoms include a foul-smelling or frothy green discharge from the vagina, vaginal itching or redness, pain during sexual intercourse, lower abdominal discomfort, and the urge to urinate. Men usually have no symptoms, but when symptoms are present, they include discharge from the urethra, the urge to urinate, and a burning sensation with urination.

trimester (try-MESS-ter). A three-month period of time. The nine months of a woman's pregnancy are divided into the first, second, and third trimesters.

tubal ligation (TOO-buhl lye-GAY-shun). A surgical procedure used to block a woman's Fallopian tubes to prevent pregnancy. Commonly referred to as "getting the tubes tied."

tubal pregnancy (TOO-buhl pregnancy). A serious condition that occurs when a fertilized egg begins to develop inside a Fallopian tube instead of inside the uterus. *See also* ectopic pregnancy.

twins. Two offspring resulting from one pregnancy. *See also* fraternal twins; identical twins.

U

ultrasound (ULL-truh-sound). Vibrations of the same physical nature as sound, but the frequencies are above the range of human hearing. Similar to an X-ray, the ultrasound has many uses, one of which is to look at a growing fetus in the womb to monitor its health and growth. It can also show the sex of the fetus and help determine when it will be born.

umbilical cord (um-BILL-ick-uhl cord). The cord that attaches an unborn baby to its mother's uterus. Through the cord, the embryo receives nourishment from the mother.

undescended testicles. A condition in which one or both of a male's testicles remain inside the body, rather than descending into the scrotum as normal. If the testicles do not descend in the first year of a boy's life, he should have an operation to bring them into the scrotum. Otherwise, the testicles may not develop properly and could also develop cancer.

ureter (you-REE-ter). A duct that carries away the urine from the kidney to the bladder.

urethra (you-REE-thra). The tube through which urine passes from the bladder during urination. In a male, sperm also is ejaculated through the urethra.

urinary opening (UR-i-ner-ee opening). The small opening at the end of the urethra where urine comes out. In the male, semen also comes out of this opening.

urinary tract infection (UR-i-ner-ee trackt infection) or **UTI**. An infection of the urinary tract that causes painful urination.

urinate (UR-i-nayt). Letting out urine from the urethra. Urine contains waste from blood that has been processed by the kidneys.

uterine contractions (YOU-ter-uhn con-TRACK-shuns). *See* contractions.

uterine lining (YOU-ter-uhn lining). *See* endometrium.

uterus (YOU-ter-us). The hollow organ in which a fertilized egg cell develops into a baby. Also called the womb.

V

vagina (va-JYE-nah). The female's major sex organ, it is a passageway leading from the uterus to the outside of a woman's body. The man's penis is inserted into the vagina during intercourse, and a baby is normally born through the vagina. *See also* sex organs.

vaginal intercourse (VAH-jin-uhl IN-ter-kors). *See* intercourse.

vaginitis (vah-jin-ITE-is). Inflammation of the vagina, often accompanied by irritation and infection.

varicocele (VAR-uh-koe-seel). An abnormal enlargement of the veins in the scrotum. It can cause pain and, in some cases, infertility. Pain can be lessened with medication, a scrotal support, or both. The condition can be surgically corrected.

vas deferens (vas DEF-er-enz). One of a pair of tubes through which sperm cells pass from the testicles.

vasectomy (vas-ECK-tuh-mee). A surgical procedure on a male that prevents sperm from moving through the vas deferens. This is a method of sterilization to prevent pregnancy.

venereal diseases (vuh-NEER-ee-uhl diseases) or **VD.** *See* sexually transmitted diseases.

vestibule (VES-teh-bule). In a female, the space between the labia minora into which the vagina and urethra open.

viable (VI-uh-bul). Able to live and develop normally. Usually refers to a baby that is able to live and grow outside the uterus.

virgin (VUR-jun). A person who has not had sexual intercourse.

virtuous (VIR-choo-us). Conforming to high principles. Often refers to being chaste or not having sexual intercourse before marriage.

voice changes. The lowering of a boy's voice, common during adolescence and caused by an increase in testosterone.

vulva (VULL-vah). The female's external sex organs. It includes the mons veneris, labia, clitoris, and vaginal opening.

W

wet dream. *See* nocturnal emission.

whole grains. Grains such as wheat, oats, and rice that have not been processed so they still contain the outer shell and the "germ" of a grain kernel. Whole grain foods provide more nourishment than processed grains and help the digestive tract.

wife. The female partner in a marriage.

withdrawal. *See* coitus interruptus.

womb (woom). *See* uterus.

Y

yeast infection (yeest infection). An infection that causes itching and burning in the vagina.

Z

zits. *See* pimples.

zygote (ZI-gote). A fertilized ovum (egg cell). This is the first stage in the development of a baby inside the mother's body. Three to four days after fertilization, the zygote develops into a morula.